70 wicked recipes

SECOND

that will leave you

HELPINGS

wanting more

LIAM CHARLES

70 wicked recipes

SECOND

that will leave you

HELPINGS

wanting more

LIAM CHARLES

HODDER &
STOUGHTON

Contents

#SecondHelpings

'Ello. I promised you there would be a sequel, and the name is pretty sick, don't you think? Okay, so the first book was straight I N D U L G E N C E. This book, however, is more balanced. From banging crowd-pleasers to comfort foods (of course) and, drum roll… healthy (-ish, lol) meals. I can assure you every book I make is never just for the sake of it. It will invite you to a particular part of my life. And currently all the recipes that are in this book are all the things I love to eat… and drink. Yup, we are talking beverages as well. Alright, let me stop waffling and give you a little breakdown of the book without giving too much away.

EQUIPMENT

The dishes in this book are, as always, fun, nostalgic and interactive. Treat them as base recipes, and once you have mastered one, run wild with it. Change the flavour, add something, change the decoration… hey, you can even make it bigger! Baking equipment can be a little intimidating, but once you have the essentials, with a few cheeky add-ons, you are good to go. This is the equipment you will need to make the dishes and bakes in this book. Remember to build up your utility belt slowly, though. Don't get everything straight away. Get confident with one or two tools, then move on. Sooner or later you will be a fully functional hero.

THE ESSENTIALS

baking trays and
  baking sheets
cake board
cake leveller
cake scraper
juicer
mixing bowls

offset palette knife
pastry cutters of
  various sizes
pie dishes (large and
  individual sizes)
pudding moulds
piping bags and nozzles

wire rack
20cm cake tin
12-hole muffin tray
30 x 20cm baking tin
900g loaf tin
1.2-litre pudding basin

THE SERIOUS STUFF

cake turntable
cannoli tubes
crumpet rings
deep-fat fryer
egg rings

electric hand-held mixer
food-processor
hinged ice-cream scoop
ice-cream machine
kitchen blowtorch

pasta machine
silicone dome mould
stand mixer
sugar thermometer

SAVOURY DISHES

AND THEY SAID I COULDN'T DO SAVOURY.

See, I don't know who actually said that, but I am going to say it anyway. The dishes in this book are wicked: well tasty, foolproof food that everyone can make. There is definitely something for everyone: my meat eaters, pescatarians, vegetarians… vegans, bear with me, give me another year or two. I got you, and I don't want you lot to be disappointed.

All the ingredients for the recipes – sweet and savoury – are easy to find, and most of them involve just your regular kitchen equipment. If you don't have the kit, I have offered alternatives, wherever possible. For example, if you don't have a deep-fat fryer, use a heavy-based saucepan and test the temperature of the oil with a food thermometer or by dropping some of the mixture into the oil and seeing how quickly it sizzles.

TEKKY LEVELS

I've categorised these a bit like video games: easy, intermediate and hard. But we are going to switch it up. The main differences between the levels is the amount of time and effort each recipe takes to make. Anyone can make them, trust me. So, to translate:

light work –
easy

you got this –
intermediate

now you're showing off –
hard

TFI: TEXTURE × FLAVOUR × INSPIRATION

If someone asks me what my philosophy is when it comes to food, I simply say "TFI". The TFI triangle in your dish or bakes is a must.

TEXTURE

This is so important to me I can't even put it into words. Well, I kinda can. I'm not a massive fan of dishes that have the same texture throughout. Food is meant to take you on a journey, it's meant to be memorable. That's why each dish has a minimum of three textures that are carefully paired together: for example, a pocket of crunchy crumble, a thin but smooth layer of jelly and soft and fluffy sponge.

FLAVOUR

Flavour: for me, it's like making a sick song. It has to have layers. You want a good baseline of primary ingredients to build on. Then the melody comes in, bringing in a little personality. This is when you decide what route you are going to go down – spicy, salty, sharp – you pick. Finally, you have the lyrics. It's the lyrics that bring all the flavours together and stick in your mind!

Take my recipe, What Came First, the Egg or the Lemon? (page 186):

× The BASELINE is the lemon
× The MELODY is the honey and herbs
× The LYRIC is the marshmallow topping

So, the next time you cook, ask yourself, what am I trying to say with this bake or dish? And then start with that baseline.

INSPIRATION

Genuine inspiration and true connection to your work will take it to the next level.
  Inspiration is the engine, it's what gets you started. I tend to draw from everyday life: what I eat on a normal day, things I see around me or what I watch on TV. Hey, it could even be as obscure as a conversation I overhear when I'm out.
  Nostalgia is a massive one for me; I have a personal bank of memories that I always refer back to – a sentimental feeling always produces something special.

"Whoa. Got a little deep there. Alright then. That's that. Come on, let me take you through the book. You might want to eat something while you're reading... I'm just saying."

Proper Meals

01

The Chicken Salad

olive oil, for cooking
2 corn cobs
100g Parmesan, grated, to serve

Chicken
4 large chicken breasts (skin on),
    cut in half lengthways to make
    8 chicken strips
1–2 tsp all-purpose seasoning,
    to taste
1–2 tsp ground cumin, to taste
1–2 tsp smoked paprika, to taste
1–2 tsp dried mixed herbs, to taste
fine sea salt, to taste
cracked black pepper, to taste

Honey × Mustard Dressing
65g mayo
3 tbsp English mustard
3 tbsp runny honey
1 tbsp cider vinegar
½ tsp cracked black pepper

Salad Base
2 large butterhead lettuces,
    washed and roughly chopped
200g mixed salad leaves, washed
20 cherry tomatoes, halved
2 tbsp chopped dill
100g sun-dried tomatoes,
    roughly chopped
2 ripe avocados, sliced

Garlic Quickie
1 small ciabatta or baguette
1 tbsp mayo
2 tbsp salted butter, softened
a small bunch of basil,
    leaves chopped
3 garlic cloves, crushed

I am a feeder and I love to make comfort food, but sometimes, especially at lunchtimes, a good salad is awesome. I'm not talking about those sad salads with just one topping, I'm talking about the ones with shed-loads of toppings, textures and colours. It's all about balance and assembling healthy wholesome ingredients, and this is one of my favourite lunches. There is a little cheeky wink here and there, but ay, come on, that's the only way salads will make it into this book. Say 'ello to The Chicken Salad.

FINGER LICKING
Put the chicken in a bowl and season it with the spices, dried herbs and some salt and pepper. Leave to sit for 15 minutes.

"Okay, with the whole seasoning thing, use your senses: smell and eye-ball the quantities. No matter how many times you season something, it will always taste different and hey, you might not want it to be as spicy as your previous batch, so express yourself."

HONEY DRESSING REHEARSAL
Combine all the dressing ingredients in a small bowl then keep in the fridge until ready to use.

CHEFFING
Heat a few splashes of olive oil in a griddle pan over a medium heat, then add the chicken and cook for 5 minutes on each side, or until cooked through.

Once all the chicken is cooked, transfer it to a plate, then add a little bit more olive oil to the griddle pan and brush it across the base so it's evenly coated. Add the corn cobs and cook them for 5 minutes, turning them so they are evenly and lightly charred. Remove from the pan, and once cooled cut the corn kernels off the cobs.

Cut the ciabatta or baguette in half lengthways, then cut each half in half again, crossways. Mix the mayo, butter, basil and garlic together thoroughly in a bowl, then generously spread each slice of bread with the mixture. Heat a little more oil in the same pan you used for the chicken and corn, over a medium heat, then place the bread face down and cook for 2–3 minutes until golden brown.

turn over

ASSEMBLE

Put all the salad base ingredients in a large bowl, apart from the avocados. Lay your chicken pieces on top of salad, followed with generous squiggles of the honey × mustard dressing. Top with the avocado and a sprinkle of Parmesan and the charred corn. Ohhhh, and don't forget that garlic bread. This salad has so many levels. I might make a book about salads next time (nahhhhhh, changed my mind).

"Throughout uni this is pretty much the only thing I would eat for lunch. Shout out to Goldsmiths Mama at the café."

Mexi Salad Bowls

Quinoa
200g quinoa, rinsed
2 spring onions, trimmed
    and chopped
100g pomegranate seeds
a handful of chopped mixed
    fresh herbs (I like to use
    coriander and parsley)

Tofu
500g tofu
5 tbsp light soy sauce
100g tomato ketchup
3 tsp mild chilli powder
3 tsp garlic powder
½ tsp cayenne pepper
2 tsp ground cumin
2 tbsp olive oil, plus extra
    for drizzling

Salad
grated zest and juice of 2 limes
2 medium mangoes, peeled
    and cubed
1 large, ripe avocado, peeled
    and diced
220g cherry tomatoes, halved
2 red chillies, seeded and
    finely chopped
2 small red onions, finely chopped
a small handful of coriander,
    leaves chopped
2 x 400g tins black beans,
    drained and rinsed

Mexi dressing
½ ripe avocado, peeled
4 tbsp orange juice
3 tsp agave syrup
3 tsp hot sauce (I like Dunn's River
    Jamaican hot sauce)
½ tsp ground cumin
½ tsp chilli powder
4 tbsp olive oil
fine sea salt, to taste
cracked black pepper, to taste

Tortilla Bowl
4 large tortilla wraps
vegetable oil, for brushing

I went to this restaurant recently and, believe it or not, I had a salad for dinner. Crazy, init? But it was packed with so many different ingredients it was banging. The best thing about it was that it was served in a tortilla bowl. I had to go home and work out how they made the bowl… clocked it!

Preheat oven to 200°C/Fan 180°C/Gas 6.

QUINOA
Put the quinoa in a large saucepan with 400ml salted water, place over a medium heat and bring to the boil. Reduce the heat, cover and simmer for 12–15 minutes, or until the quinoa is tender and fluffy, the grains look like they are just about to burst, and the water has evaporated. Drain well and tip into a bowl. Stir the spring onion, pomegranate seeds and mixed herbs into the quinoa while it's still warm and set to the side.

TOFU
Break up the tofu into chunky pieces in a large bowl, then add all the remaining ingredients and stir until well combined.

Drizzle some olive oil over a baking tray, spread the tofu over the tray and bake for 25 minutes, turning the tofu halfway through, until golden brown.

SALAD × MEXI DRESSING
While the tofu is cooking, combine all the salad ingredients in a bowl. Put all the dressing ingredients in the bowl of a food-processor or blender and blitz until smooth. Transfer to a bowl and feel free to adjust the sweetness or heat by adding a little more hot sauce or syrup.

'TILLA BOWLS
Lightly brush one side of a tortilla wrap with vegetable oil. Press the tortilla into an ovenproof bowl, oiled side down, so that it takes the shape of the bowl, then lightly brush the other side with oil. Repeat this process with the rest of the tortillas. Bake for 8–10 minutes, until golden and crispy.

ASSEMBLE
Combine the quinoa and the salad and gently stir, then fill each tortilla bowl with the salad. Top each serving with a few tofu pieces and, finally, the Mexi dressing.

Proper Meals

Veggie Wedgie Pie

1 red onion, thinly sliced
60g small broccoli florets
1 red or yellow and 1 green pepper, seeded and cut into chunks
2 courgettes, thickly sliced
1 large sweet potato, peeled and thinly sliced
1 tsp ground cumin
3 tbsp olive oil
250g hummus
2 tsp harissa paste
1 tbsp pomegranate molasses
grated zest of 1 unwaxed lemon
1 tbsp chopped fresh coriander leaves
2 × 375g packs ready-rolled puff pastry
1 large egg, beaten
fine sea salt, to taste
cracked black pepper, to taste

On my mum's side of the family there are a few who don't eat loads of meat. I haven't made this one for them yet, but this super simple pie is filled with veg and it's proper tasty so I know my family will love it. I tell you what: cut a naughty wedge of it, pop it in a container with a bit of salad, and it's a perfect lunch.

ROAST
Preheat oven to 220°C/Fan 200°C/Gas 7.

Mix the onion, broccoli florets, peppers, courgettes and sweet potato in a roasting tin, add the cumin and olive oil, season with salt and pepper and toss well to coat. Roast for 25–30 minutes.

MIX × LINE × LAY
While the vegetables are roasting, mix the hummus in a bowl with the harissa paste, pomegranate molasses, lemon zest and coriander.

Remove the vegetables from the oven and reduce the oven temperature to 200°C/Fan 180°C/Gas 6. Unroll both sheets of pastry so you have two rectangles. Lay one piece on a baking sheet lined with baking paper and spread the hummus mixture evenly over it, leaving a 2cm border around the edge. Cover the hummus with slightly overlapping layers of roast sweet potato. Pile on the rest of the roasted veggies.

"The only border control I believe in."

"W" FOR WEDGIE AND WINNING
Brush the border with the beaten egg, then roll the other pastry sheet out just a little thinner than the first piece. Cut the letter "W" out of the middle of the pastry. Place it over the filling and gently press the pastry edges together with a fork to seal.

Trim off any excess pastry. Brush the top of the pie with beaten egg.

BAKE
Bake the pie for 30 minutes, or until the pastry is golden brown and well puffed up. Remove from the oven and serve it warm or at room temperature.

"Oooh, look at you flexing that veggie muscle."

Proper Meals

Serves 4   Skill Level: light work   You will need 4 x 18cm square
                                                          or round baking tins, or 2 large
                                                          40 x 30cm roasting tins

Monday Roast Wraps

Proper Meals

Cheeky Add-on Veg
1 broccoli head, cut into florets
2 tbsp olive oil
2 garlic cloves, thinly sliced
1 tsp dried chilli flakes
250g parsnips, peeled and
    quartered lengthways
250g carrots, peeled and
    quartered lengthways
4 tbsp plain flour
1 tbsp runny honey
2 tbsp sunflower oil
30g unsalted butter
fine sea salt, to taste
cracked black pepper, to taste

Yorkshire Wrap
300g plain flour
6 large eggs
600ml whole milk
1 tsp fine sea salt
125g mature Cheddar, grated
20g chives, snipped
6 tbsp vegetable oil

Leftover Fillings
8 tbsp cranberry sauce
400g leftover roast beef,
    chicken or lamb, sliced
200ml leftover gravy, warmed up
mustard, to taste (optional)

It's a tradition, it's loved by millions, it's the roast dinner. Every single household in the UK has their own interpretation of this classic family meal. And we all, without a shadow of a doubt, cook way too much then go back for 'round two' the next day, but here is the switch up: why serve 'round two' on a plate? Make a Yorkshire pudding wrap! Chuck in your leftover meat and gravy and some of my cheeky add-ons (or just leftover veg) and we're good to go. Nice one.

Preheat oven to 190°C/Fan 170°C/Gas 5.

CHEEKY ADD-ONS
Bring a large pan of salted water to the boil. Add the broccoli and cook for 5–7 minutes until just tender. While it's cooking, heat the olive oil in a large frying pan over a medium heat, pop in the garlic and cook until lightly golden. Drain the broccoli well, then toss it into the pan of garlicky oil and add the chilli flakes. Season with salt and pepper and remove from the heat.

Bring the same large pan to the boil with fresh salted water. Add the parsnips and carrots and cook for 6 minutes, then drain and allow them to steam dry.

Sprinkle the flour over the veg and drizzle over the honey, then toss to coat. Put the veg into a roasting tin with the sunflower oil and butter then roast for 40 minutes, turning them after 20 minutes, until the parsnips are golden. Pop the roasted veg into a dish until ready to serve.

YORKSHIRE WRAPS
While the carrots and parsnips are roasting, whisk the flour, eggs, milk and salt in a bowl or jug until smooth. Whisk in the cheese and chives, cover with clingfilm and leave the mixture to rest for 30 minutes.

Once the carrots and parsnips are ready, increase the oven temperature to 220°C/Fan 200°C/Gas 7.

Divide the vegetable oil between the four individual baking tins or two large roasting tins and put them in the oven for about 15 minutes. Once hot, remove the tins and divide the Yorkshire pudding mixture between them. Return to the oven and cook until puffed-up and golden – 15 minutes if you're using 4 smaller tins, 25 minutes if you're using the larger tins.

turn over

ASSEMBLE

Once the Yorkshires are done, quickly remove them from their tins and flatten. If you have baked two larger Yorkshires, then cut them in half. Spread 2 tablespoons of cranberry sauce over one half of each flattened Yorkshire, followed by meat slices, broccoli, parsnips, carrots and gravy.

Now roll up and serve your Sunday... sorry, Monday... roast wrap.

TIP

OHHHHH I tell you what, if you have any roast potatoes or pigs in blankets, throw them in! Hey, my nan even makes mac 'n' cheese with the Sunday dinner. GO WILD!

Game Station Pie

Fish Filling
70g salted butter
1 large leek, trimmed, washed
    and chopped
2 shallots, chopped
1 small onion, chopped
100g mushrooms, chopped
400ml whole milk, plus extra
    if needed
300ml double cream
3 bay leaves
900g fish fillets (combination
    of haddock, cod, salmon)
150g cooked jumbo prawns
50g plain flour
a small bunch of fresh flat-leaf
    parsley, finely chopped
nutmeg, freshly grated, to taste
fine sea salt, to taste
cracked black pepper, to taste

Herby Pastry
525g plain flour, plus extra
    for dusting
1 tsp fine sea salt
135g unsalted butter, cold, diced
135g lard, cold, diced
2 tbsp fresh herbs (e.g.
    thyme, rosemary, or sage,
    or a mixture), finely chopped
4½ tbsp cold water
1 large egg, beaten

Now, I'm going to be honest with you: I didn't have loads
of fish pies when I was growing up. Recently I had one in a
pub and realised I wasn't a fan, but experiences like this just
encourage me to make new things. I thought, "How could
I make a great version of this?"

FISH FILLING
Melt 20g of the butter in a saucepan over a medium heat. Add
the leek, shallots, onion and mushrooms, season with salt and
pepper, then cook, stirring, for 3–4 minutes until soft.

Put the milk, double cream, bay leaves and fish in a wide, shallow
pan, place over a medium heat, bring the liquid just to the boil,
then reduce the heat and simmer gently for 10 minutes or until
the fish is just cooked. Transfer the fish to a plate to cool and strain
the liquid into a heatproof jug.

Flake the fish into a bowl once it's cooled, removing any skin and
bones. Stir in the prawns and cooked vegetables.

Melt the remaining 50g of butter in a saucepan over a medium
heat, stir in the flour and cook it for a minute, then take off the
heat and gradually stir in the warm milk. Return the pan to the
heat and cook the sauce over a medium-low heat for 10 minutes,
stirring, until it has slightly thickened. Remove from the heat, stir
in the parsley and season to taste with salt, pepper and nutmeg.
Add more milk if it's too thick.

Pour three-quarters of the sauce over the fish mixture then spoon
it into the pie dish. Pour over the rest of the sauce and set the dish
aside to allow the filling to cool.

HERBY CRUST
To make the pastry, sift the flour then add it to the bowl of a
food-processor along with the salt, butter, lard and herbs. Pulse
until the mixture resembles fine breadcrumbs. While the motor
is running, add the water and pulse again until the dough comes
together to form a rough ball.

Tip the dough onto a lightly floured surface and gently knead
until smooth.

Roll the pastry on a lightly floured surface to a thickness of 5mm,
about 2.5cm larger in diameter than the top of the pie dish.

Proper Meals

turn over

ASSEMBLE

Cut a 2cm-wide strip around the edge of the pastry, then press it onto the rim of the pie dish. Brush the pastry with beaten egg and gently lift the pastry lid onto the dish. Press the pastry edges together to seal, then trim away any excess pastry and crimp the edges between your fingers.

Preheat oven to 200°C/Fan 180°C/Gas 6.

Re-roll the leftover pastry to make the decorations for the pie. You need a thin 16cm circle, 2 x 5cm circles, a 2–3cm square, a 2–3cm circle and 2 × 2–3cm triangles. Place the largest circle directly in the centre of the pie. Place the two triangles in each of the top corners, the 5cm circles in each of the bottom corners, and the smallest circle and square just slightly above the 5cm circles.

Cut out a "G", "S" and a "P" and place on top of the largest circle, in the centre of the pie.

BAKE

Brush the top of the pie with beaten egg and bake for 30 minutes until golden brown. Remove from the oven and serve.

So there we have the complete picture: we had the controllers in my first book, and now we have the game station. A whole gaming experience in pie form.

TIP
Don't forget to always taste as you go, to check for seasoning.

"Ever wondered what the Pie 'n' Play pies from *Cheeky Treats* are connected to? Behold the Game Station Pie. Pretty sick, init."

Sliding into the VMs

Patties
600g raw beetroots, peeled
    and grated
grated zest and juice of
    2 unwaxed lemons
a small bunch of spring onions,
    trimmed and thinly sliced
2 tsp fennel seeds
3 garlic cloves, finely chopped
a small bunch of mint, leaves
    stripped and finely chopped
6 tbsp plain flour
2 large eggs
olive oil, for frying
fine sea salt, to taste
cracked black pepper, to taste

To Serve
hummus
pickled gherkins
mixed salad
6 burger buns

I've had a lot of direct messages, or "DMs", from vegetarians, asking me for some veggie recipes, so this one is for those "VM"ers. AYYY, I have to hook up my vegetarian pals, and I actually have a few so, you guys, if you don't like this one I'm going to be really upset. The amount of beetroot I ate to get this one right was insane.

PATTIES
Preheat oven to 200°C/Fan 180°C/Gas 6.

Wrap the grated beetroot in a clean cloth, tea towel or piece of muslin and squeeze to remove as much juice from the beetroot as possible. Put it in a bowl, add the lemon juice and a pinch of salt and leave to sit for 1 hour, then strain, return to the bowl and add the spring onion, fennel seeds, garlic, mint and lemon zest. Add 3 tablespoons of the flour and the eggs, and season with salt and pepper. Mix until well combined. Form the mixture into 6 patties then coat them in the rest of the flour.

Heat a large frying pan over a medium-high heat, add a couple splashes of olive oil, then fry the patties for 4 minutes on each side.

Transfer the patties to a baking tray and pop in the oven for 10–15 minutes until they are cooked through and the outside is crisp.

ASSEMBLE
Place a generous helping of hummus, pickles and salad on the base of each bun, then add a beetroot patty and close with the bun lid.

"Short, simple, healthy... Sometimes that's what you want in life, you know."

Proper Meals

The Mac Attack

"CFS"
400g sweet potatoes,
    peeled and diced
3 tbsp olive oil
150g good-quality cooking
    chorizo, thinly sliced
150g feta, crumbled
fine sea salt, to taste
cracked black pepper, to taste

Macaroni Base
20g unsalted butter
30g plain flour
300ml whole milk
560g mature Cheddar, grated
1 tsp English mustard
700g macaroni

"Taco Maco"
1 tbsp olive oil
½ red pepper, seeded and diced
½ yellow pepper, seeded and diced
½ red onion, chopped
1 x 200g tin mixed beans,
    drained and rinsed
1 tsp smoked paprika
1 heaped tbsp tomato
    and chilli chutney
15g tortilla chips
10g mature Cheddar, grated

Salmon × Cream Cheese Bagel
120g thinly sliced smoked salmon
10g dill, leaves picked and chopped
100g cream cheese
1 tbsp garlic oil
100g bagel or bread
    croutons (optional)

"Cheeseboard"
25g mature Cheddar, grated
50g mozzarella, torn into chunks
25g Gruyère, grated
25g Parmesan, grated
4 tbsp sandwich pickle (optional)
5 multigrain crackers (optional)

Ever since we were young, macaroni cheese has been mine and my brother's all-time favourite dish, but as I've got older I've tried new foods and been inspired by wicked flavour combinations that captured my imagination. And here they all are, in one dish! First off, the "Taco Maco" Mexican-inspired corner, with spicy beans and tortilla chips, then "CFS", the sweet salty corner flavoured with chorizo, feta and sweet potato. Next, we take a trip down to Brick Lane, inspired by a place that probably make the best cream cheese and smoked salmon bagels in London. Finally, we have the "Cheeseboard": four cheeses of glory, topped off with classic crackers. Ooooh, and there's one more surprise to add to that corner – read the recipe and find out what it is. Trust me, it works.

Preheat oven to 220°C/Fan 200°C/Gas 7.

CFS STEP I
Mix the sweet potatoes for the CFS topping with the olive oil and some salt and pepper in a shallow roasting tin. Roast in the oven, turning frequently so they don't burn, for 15–20 minutes until the sweet potato has softened, then remove from the oven and set to one side.

Reduce the oven temperature to 200°C/Fan 180°C/Gas 6.

SAUCY CHEESE BASE × PASTA
Melt the butter for the macaroni base in a large saucepan over a medium heat. Stir in the flour and cook the mixture for 2 minutes or so, then gradually add the milk, stirring, until you have a smooth sauce. Simmer gently for 8 minutes, stirring constantly, until thickened. Now for the good bit – add the Cheddar and stir until melted. Add the mustard, stir again, then remove from the heat.

Meanwhile, cook the macaroni in a large pan of salted boiling water for 8 minutes, so that it retains some bite, then drain. Stir the pasta into the cheese sauce and pour the mixture into the ovenproof dish. Set aside.

turn over

"TACO MACO"

To make the Taco Maco topping, heat the olive oil in a large frying pan over a medium-high heat. Add the peppers and onion and fry for 5–10 minutes, until softened. Toss in the mixed beans followed by the smoked paprika and chutney and cook, stirring, for 2–3 minutes. Season with salt and pepper to taste.

Top one quarter of the macaroni cheese with the bean mixture, then wedge in the tortilla chips and sprinkle over the grated Cheddar. Set aside.

CFS STEP II

Heat a dry frying pan over a medium heat, add the sliced chorizo and fry for 5–10 minutes, until the chorizo releases its oil and crisps up. Spoon the chorizo and the oil over another quarter of the macaroni cheese, add the sweet potato chunks then sprinkle over the crumbled feta. Set aside again.

SALMON × CREAM CHEESE BAGEL

Top a third quarter of the macaroni cheese with the slices of smoked salmon and sprinkle over the dill. Create four decent-sized pockets in the macaroni cheese mixture then place dollops of cream cheese into them. Drizzle with the garlic oil. Set aside again.

"CHEESEBOARD"

Use the four cheeses for the remaining quarter, gently mixing each one, except the Parmesan, into the final quarter of the dish. Sprinkle over the Parmesan.

Bake the topped macaroni cheese for 20 minutes, until golden. Remove from the oven and allow to rest for 5 minutes, then finish off the four-cheeses quarter with a few teaspoons of pickle and some broken-up multigrain crackers (if using), then sprinkle the salmon and cream cheese bagel with the bagel croutons if you wish. Serve with a massive salad.

TIP

What's great about this recipe is that it's sooooooo versatile. What are your favourite things to eat? Sweet or savoury, if you add them to the base of this mac × cheese you could be onto something!

Snuggly Veggie Cannelloni

500g dried cannelloni pasta tubes
100g Parmesan, grated, plus
    an extra handful for sprinkling
fine sea salt, to taste
cracked black pepper, to taste
mixed salad, to serve

Veggie Beany Chilli
3 tbsp olive oil
1 large onion, chopped
1 celery stick, finely chopped
1 medium carrot, finely chopped
1 yellow pepper, seeded and
    finely chopped
1 x 460g jar roasted red peppers
1 tsp chipotle paste
1 tbsp red wine vinegar
1 tbsp smoked paprika
3 tsp ground cumin
½ tsp ground cinnamon
1 tbsp dried mixed herbs
2 x 400g tins chopped tomatoes
200g refried beans
1 x 400g tin kidney beans,
    drained and rinsed
1 x 400g tin black beans,
    drained and rinsed

Meat-free, packed with veggies and beans, this is a wholesome meal for any day of the week. Oh yeah, and your pasta shells are baked vertically – it's pretty cool.

CHILLI
Heat the olive oil in a large, heavy-based saucepan over a medium heat. Pop the onion, celery, carrot and yellow pepper into the pan and fry gently for 10 minutes until the veg has softened.

Drain the jar of peppers over a bowl, making sure you're catching the juices. Put half the jarred peppers in the bowl of a food-processor with the chipotle paste, red wine vinegar, dried spices and herbs, and whizz to a smooth paste (or do this with a stick blender), then stir the paste into the softened veg and cook for a couple minutes.

Add the tinned tomatoes and refried beans to the saucepan with half a tin of water and the reserved jarred pepper juices. Cover and simmer gently for 1 hour, stirring occasionally, until thickened.

Finally, stir in the remaining peppers and the kidney and black beans, and cook for a further 10 minutes. Season to taste with salt and pepper.

Preheat oven to 200°C/Fan 180°C/Gas 6.

COOK THE TUBES
Bring a large saucepan of salted water to the boil. Add a few cannelloni tubes at a time, stirring occasionally, and par-cook them for 5–7 minutes. Lift them out with a slotted spoon and cool under cold running water just until you can handle them. Put the par-cooked pasta in a large bowl with the 100g grated Parmesan and mix gently with your hands until is well coated.

ASSEMBLE
Spread a ladleful of veggie chilli at the bottom of the large casserole dish or cake tin. Place the pasta tubes in the dish or tin vertically.

"Snuggly cannelloni."

Once the pasta is tightly packed in the dish or tin, pour the remaining veggie chilli over the pasta and gently press the sauce into the holes. Sprinkle more Parmesan over the top and bake for 30 minutes until golden and crispy on top.

Remove from the oven and allow to cool slightly, then serve with some mixed salad. Ahhh. I tell you what… if you wait a little longer it could be sliceable!

Proper Meals

Super Salmon Noodle Salad

Salmon
4 salmon fillets (skin on)
10cm piece fresh root ginger,
    peeled and roughly chopped
3 garlic cloves, roughly chopped
3 tbsp light soy sauce
1 tbsp tamarind paste
juice of 2 limes
1 tbsp basil leaves
olive oil, for frying
50g unsalted butter

Pickled Cucumber Salad
1 large cucumber
¼ large onion, thinly sliced
30ml rice vinegar
2 tbsp toasted sesame
    seeds
1 tsp fine sea salt
1 tsp caster sugar
½ tsp dried chilli flakes

Dressing
juice of 2 limes
1 tbsp light soy sauce
1 garlic clove, crushed
1 tbsp finely grated fresh
    root ginger
2 tbsp soft light brown sugar
2 tbsp fish sauce

Noodle Salad
300g rice noodles
3 spring onions, trimmed
    and thinly sliced
2 large carrots, julienned
1 tbsp chopped basil leaves
2 tbsp chopped mint leaves
2 tbsp chopped coriander leaves

To Serve
75g roasted cashews,
    roughly crushed

Love a good chunk of salmon, I do. Serve it with a banging noodle salad, topped off with fresh pickled cucumber, and it's perfect for a light dinner (always make sure you have room for dessert, that's what I say). The name of this recipe is also a bit of a tongue twister – try saying it three times without fluffing it!

SALMON I
Put the salmon fillets in a bowl. Pop the rest of the ingredients for the salmon (except the oil and butter) into the bowl of a food-processor and blitz to a smooth paste. Tip the paste over the salmon, then use your hands to gently rub it in. Cover and put in the fridge for at least 1 hour to marinate (you can leave it for a few hours or overnight if you like).

PICKLED CUCUMBER
Cut off both ends of the cucumber, then use a vegetable peeler to peel the cucumber into long, thin strips. Put the strips into a bowl with the onion. Combine the rest of the pickled cucumber ingredients then drizzle over the cucumber and onion and set aside until ready to use.

SALMON II
Heat a couple of splashes of olive oil in a large non-stick frying pan over a medium heat and add the butter. Swirl the butter around the pan until it has melted and is foaming. Turn up the heat and place the salmon in the pan skin side down. Cook for about 7 minutes, until the skin is crisp, then flip the fillets over, reduce the heat and cook for a further 3 minutes, or until cooked through. Transfer the salmon to a plate and drizzle the buttery juices over it.

DRESSING × NOODLE SALAD
To make the dressing, place all the ingredients in the bowl of a food-processor or a blender and blitz until well combined. Transfer to a bowl.

Put the noodles in a heatproof bowl. Pour over enough boiling water to cover and soak according to the packet instructions, then drain well, put them into a serving bowl, drizzle with about half the dressing and leave to sit for 10 minutes.

Add the rest of the salad ingredients to the noodles and mix again until well combined.

ASSEMBLE
Here's the best bit. Break the salmon into large chunks, toss them into the noodles and combine well. Top with pickled cucumber, then finish with a drizzle of the dressing and the cashews.

Coronation the Chicken Pie

Proper Meals

Pastry
570g plain flour, plus
    extra for dusting
4 tsp ground turmeric
3 tsp dried mixed herbs
200g lard
200ml water
1 large egg, beaten

Filling
4 boneless chicken breasts, skin
    removed, cut into cubes
4 boneless chicken thighs,
    skin removed, cut into cubes
40g fresh coriander
2 tsp ground coriander
2 tsp ground cumin
1 tsp ground turmeric
3 tsp garam masala
1 tsp mild curry powder
1 red chilli, seeded and
    finely chopped
juice of 2 limes
100g sultanas

Mango × Lime Jelly
3 gelatine leaves
250ml mango juice
grated zest and juice of 1 lime

So, this recipe is inspired by a recent memory: going to see one of the most hotly anticipated films this year, my pals and I went to a local supermarket to get help-yourself salad tubs. Babs, one of my mates, had so much bloody coronation chicken in his tub he couldn't even close it. I was never keen on it, but hey, why not, let's try a bit. I had it… I was sold. Come on then, let's slap it in a pie and see if my pals like it.

DAY I

SEASON CHICKEN
Preheat oven to 190°C/Fan 170°C/Gas 5.

Put the meat in a bowl, chuck in all the other ingredients for the chicken filling, stir, cover and leave in the fridge to chill until ready to use.

PASTRY
To make the pastry, pop the flour, turmeric and dried mixed herbs in a large bowl. Put the lard and water in a small saucepan and place over a low heat. Gently heat until the lard melts. Bring the mixture just to the boil, then remove from the heat and stir it into the flour using a spoon. When the mixture is cool enough to touch, knead it well until the pastry is smooth. Cut off a quarter of the dough for the lid, wrap it in clingfilm and put it in the fridge.

ASSEMBLE × BAKE
Working quickly, roll the larger piece of dough on a floured surface to make a large 30cm circle that's 5mm thick, then place it in the base of the springform cake tin. Working while the dough is still pliable, press it evenly over the base and up the sides of the tin.

"Please make sure there are no holes — we don't want a leaking pie."

Fill the pie with the chilled meat mixture, pressing it down gently to pack it in well. Roll out the rest of the dough for the lid, to a diameter of 20cm and thickness of 5mm. Pop the pastry lid on top of the pie, trim away the excess and pinch the edges of the pastry together.

turn over

Make a small hole in the centre of the pie for steam to escape from, using a knife or the handle of a wooden spoon.

Use the excess pastry you've trimmed away to cut out a crown, using a knife. Place it on top of the pie, positioning it just next to the steam hole (the steam hole mustn't be covered).

Brush the top with the beaten egg and bake for 1 hour, or until a food thermometer inserted into the pie reads 75°C. Remove from the oven, leave to cool, then chill overnight.

DAY II
The next morning, soak the gelatine leaves in a bowl of cold water for 5 minutes to soften.

Heat half the mango and all the lime juice and zest in a small pan until warm. Squeeze the excess water from the gelatine leaves then stir them into the juice until dissolved. Add the remaining mango juice. Use a funnel inserted into the steam hole to slowly pour the juice into the pie. Chill the pie in the fridge for a couple more hours to allow time for the jelly to set, then remove it from the tin and get slicing!

Well Lazy Wellington

Ruff Puff
125g plain flour, plus extra
    for dusting
125g strong white flour
1 tsp fine sea salt
½ tsp finely ground black pepper
½ tsp ground cloves
250g unsalted butter, cold,
    cut into small chunks
140–150ml cold water
1 large egg, lightly beaten

Garlicky Butter
100g salted butter, slightly softened
a handful of parsley leaves,
    finely chopped
2 small garlic cloves, crushed
juice of 1 lemon

Wellington Toppers
12 slices prosciutto, finely chopped
4 tbsp olive oil
400g chestnut mushrooms,
    finely chopped
large sprig of thyme
4 x 200g beef steaks (sirloin,
    or your favourite cut)
90g salted butter
fine sea salt, to taste
cracked black pepper, to taste

To Serve
mashed or roast potatoes
salad
shop-bought peppercorn
    sauce (optional)

The beef Wellington is an absolute classic, but it can be a little time-consuming and tricky to make sure the pastry is well baked and the beef is cooked just right. This simplified version will get rid of those worries and most definitely go down a Wellington storm. Yup, the recipe does require you to make your pastry, but it's so worth it! Have a go.

RUFF PUFF I

Sift both flours into a bowl along with the salt, black pepper and ground cloves. Give it a quick stir. Now roughly…

Rub the chunks of butter into the flour loosely with your fingertips – you want to keep some small bits of butter.

Make a well in the middle of the bowl and gradually pour in about two-thirds of the water, mixing continuously with a butter knife until it comes together to form a firm dough, adding more of the water if necessary.

Bring the dough together into a ball, wrap it in clingfilm and place in the fridge to chill for 30 minutes.

GARLICKY BUTTER

While the pastry is chilling, move on to the butter. Mash all the ingredients together in a bowl, adding a generous amount of cracked black pepper, then squash the butter between two sheets of clingfilm, wrap it up and put it in the fridge to chill.

RUFF PUFF II

Unwrap the dough, turn it out onto a lightly floured surface and knead it gently into a rectangle shape. Roll the dough in one direction until it is about 20cm wide and 50cm long. You want to keep that streaked marbled effect from the butter in the dough, so be gentle with it. Remember to keep the edges straight and even.

Fold the top third down to the centre, then the bottom third up over that. Wrap it in clingfilm and pop it in the fridge for another 20 minutes.

Unwrap the chilled pastry dough, give it a quarter turn (to the right) so you're rolling it out in different direction, and roll it out again to the original length of 20 x 50cm. Fold as before, wrap in clingfilm and chill in the fridge for another 20 minutes.

turn over

Preheat oven to 220°C/Fan 200°C/Gas 7 and line a baking sheet with baking paper.

Roll the pastry out to a large 30 x 20cm rectangle about 1.5cm thick. Place it on the lined baking sheet, brush the surface of the pastry with beaten egg and bake for 20 minutes or until the pastry is puffed and golden brown.

WELLINGTON TOPPERS
Place a large, dry frying pan over a medium heat, add the prosciutto and cook until crisp. Remove from the pan and set aside.

Add a couple of splashes of the olive oil to the same frying pan, place over a medium heat, add the mushrooms and thyme and fry for about 10 minutes until softened. Remove from the pan, discard the thyme sprig and set aside.

COOK THAT STEAK
Season the steaks with salt and pepper. Wipe the pan clean with kitchen paper, heat it until smoking hot, then add the butter and swirl until it has fully melted. Add the steaks to the pan.

How you cook your steak is entirely up to you – for a steak that's 1.5–2cm thick, cook for 2 minutes on each side for rare, but if you don't want your steak to be mooing add an extra minute of cooking time for each side to increase its doneness.

Once the steak is cooked to your liking, remove from the heat and allow to rest before slicing.

ASSEMBLE (WELL, KIND OF)
Place the cooked pastry slab on a board and top it with the mushrooms. Cut the rested steaks into 1cm-thick slices and scatter the slices across the mushrooms. Top with the prosciutto, then finally get that garlic butter you made earlier and dot little chunks around your dinner.

"Nice one. This is where you can add mashed potatoes to the club, a bit of peppercorn sauce... roast potatoes... it's up to you. ENJOY."

CL (Carrot × Lentil) Soup

Blue Cheese × Walnut Scone Crumb
240g plain flour, plus extra
   for dusting
1 tbsp baking powder
½ tsp fine sea salt
65g unsalted butter, cold, diced
a small bunch of parsley,
   finely chopped
100g blue cheese, cubed
80g walnuts, roughly chopped
55ml whole milk
2 large eggs

Soup
3 tsp cumin seeds
generous pinch of dried
   chilli flakes
900g carrots, grated
220g split red lentils
1.5 litres hot vegetable stock
200ml whole milk
fine sea salt, to taste
cracked black pepper, to taste

To Serve
crème fraîche
chilli oil
a handful of coriander leaves

Yes, CL in the periodic table is chlorine, but I can assure you, this isn't a chlorine soup. It's carrot, coriander and red lentil soup with the tastiest blue cheese scone crumb: super simple, comforting and an absolute heart warmer.

SCONES
Preheat oven to 170°C/Fan 150°C/Gas 3 and line a baking tray with baking paper.

Sift your flour and baking powder together into a large bowl and add the salt. Add the butter, then use your fingertips to rub the butter into the flour until the mixture resembles breadcrumbs. Once the butter is rubbed in, add the parsley, quickly stirring until evenly distributed, then finally add the cubed blue cheese and the walnuts. Make a well in the mixture.

Beat the milk and one of the eggs together in a jug then pour this into the scone mixture, stirring as you go. Bring the mixture together to form a rough dough (avoid over-mixing the dough).

Dust your worktop and rolling pin with flour then roll out the dough to a rough 15cm square about 2cm thick. Dip a 4cm round cutter in flour then use it to cut out as many scones as you can, using a swift motion. Lightly re-roll the leftover dough and cut out more scones until you have about 20 in total. Place the scones on the lined baking tray.

Beat the remaining egg. Using a pastry brush, slather the tops of your scones with the beaten egg. Bake for 15 minutes until well risen. The base should be a deep, golden brown, and they should sound hollow when tapped. Remove from the oven and transfer to a wire rack to cool.

turn over

Proper Meals

SOUP

Put the cumin seeds and chilli flakes in a large saucepan and heat for a couple minutes.

"You should be able to smell the aromas of the spices or see them jump up like popcorn."

Tip out half of the seeds and chilli and set them aside, then add the grated carrots, red lentils, the veggie stock and the milk to the saucepan and bring to a gentle boil. Reduce the heat and simmer for 20–30 minutes until the lentils have softened. Remove from the heat and whizz the soup in a food-processor until smooth, or use a stick blender. Season with salt and pepper to taste.

Serve the soup in bowls, finished with a generous dollop of crème fraîche, and place a couple of scones in each bowl, along with a little chilli oil squiggle. Sprinkle with coriander leaves and scatter over the remaining cumin seeds and chilli.

Lovely, quick, simple, proper tasty.

"You'll have some scones left over but don't worry, they keep in an airtight container for 2-3 days. Toast them and enjoy with some butter, or why not pop some ham in there and have a mini scone sandwich?"

Roasted × Toasted Salad

Roasted Butternut Squash
2 large butternut squash, peeled
  and cut into large 1cm-thick
  rounds, then semi-circles
4 tbsp olive oil
fine sea salt, to taste
cracked black pepper, to taste

Honey-roasted Apples
3 Granny Smith apples,
  cored and diced
1 Braeburn apple, cored
  and diced
2 tbsp lemon juice
45g unsalted butter
1 tsp fine sea salt
80ml runny honey

Honey × Lemon Dressing
2 tbsp runny honey
4 tbsp lemon juice
4 tbsp olive oil
1 tsp Dijon mustard

Salad
150g pecans
olive oil, for frying
200g unsmoked bacon lardons
200g rocket
120g goat's cheese

What makes this salad so tasty is that most of the ingredients are roasted and toasted. The depth of flavour, crispness, nuttiness and the variety of textures are to live for.

ROASTED SQUASH
Preheat oven to 220°C/Fan 200°C/Gas 7.

Put the butternut squash in a bowl, drizzle with the oil, and season with salt and pepper. Toss lightly and tip into a baking tray. Spread them out and roast for 25 minutes, then flip the squash pieces over and roast for a further 10 minutes or until golden and crisp.

ROASTED APPLES × DRESSING
Pop the diced apple into a bowl, add the lemon juice and toss. Heat a frying pan over a medium-high heat and add the butter. As soon as the butter starts to brown, add the apple and the salt to the pan. Sauté for 6 minutes, or until the edges of the apples begin to brown. Pop the apples in a baking tray, add the honey, toss to coat and bake for 10 minutes. Keep an eye on it though – you want the apples to be richly caramelised, not mushy.

Take the apple out of the baking tray and set aside (try not to smash 'em).

For the dressing, combine all the ingredients in a jar with some salt and pepper, seal and shake until well combined.

TOASTED NUTS × LARDONS
Toast the pecans in a dry frying pan over a medium heat for 5 minutes, or until your kitchen begins to smell nutty.

Transfer the pecans to a plate or bowl. Add a drizzle of oil into the pan, place over a medium heat, add the lardons and fry for 5 minutes until golden and crisp. Transfer to a plate lined with kitchen paper, to absorb excess fat.

ASSEMBLE
Break up the goat's cheese into small chunks. Place everything in a large bowl, reserving some of the lardons, pecans, roasted apples and goat's cheese. Drizzle with most of the dressing and gently toss.

Transfer the salad to a large serving plate, top with the remaining lardons, pecans, goat's cheese and apples, and finish it off with the rest of the dressing.

Proper Meals

Cottage Cheeseburger Pie

The "Patty"
3 tbsp olive oil
1 onion, roughly chopped
1 red onion, chopped
1 tomato, chopped
750g beef mince
3 tbsp tomato purée
1 tbsp English mustard
1 tbsp plain flour
4 sprigs of fresh thyme, leaves
    picked and chopped
4 sprigs of fresh flat-leaf parsley,
    leaves picked and chopped
550ml beef stock
4 pickled gherkins, roughly chopped
fine sea salt, to taste
cracked black pepper, to taste

"Chips" Topping
750g sweet potatoes, peeled
    and cut into chunks
750g King Edward potatoes,
    peeled and cut into chunks
100ml whole milk
130g salted butter
1 tbsp dried mixed herbs
3 tsp smoked paprika
150g mature Cheddar, grated
a handful of sesame seeds

Give me a proper beef burger with all the trimmings: gherkins, onions, ketchup, mustard, cheese, maybe potato fries two ways… but in the form of a cottage pie… I'm there.

THE "PATTY"

Heat half the olive oil in large frying pan over a medium heat. Add the onions and tomato and cook for 7–10 minutes until softened, then tip onto a plate.

Pop the pan back over the heat and add the rest of the oil. As soon as it's hot, add the beef mince and fry for 5–6 minutes until browned, breaking it up with a wooden spoon as it cooks. Stir in the cooked onion and tomato mixture, tomato purée and mustard and cook for a couple minutes, then add the flour and cook for another minute, stirring, before adding the thyme and parsley.

Add the beef stock and gherkins and simmer for 35 minutes, stirring occasionally, until the mince is tender and the mixture has thickened. Season to taste with salt and pepper, then remove from the heat and leave the lid on to keep it warm.

THE "CHIPS"

For the mash, put the potatoes in two separate pans of salted water and bring to the boil. Reduce the heat and simmer gently for 18–20 minutes or until both potatoes are tender. Drain and return each type of potato to their pans. Pop the pans back over the heat for 1 minute – this helps the moisture to evaporate, making a fluffier mash. Preheat oven to 220°C/Fan 200°C/Gas 7 or set your grill to medium-hot.

Mash both the potatoes well. Add the milk and 80g of the butter to the white potatoes and mash until combined, then stir through the mixed herbs. Add the remaining 50g butter to the sweet potatoes and combine, then add the smoked paprika. Season both pans of mash with salt and pepper.

ASSEMBLE

Divide the beef mince between the 6 enamel tins or 1 large dish and top with both mashes, covering half the mince with one mash and the rest with the other mash, giving it a bit of a swirl to create a slight ripple effect (careful not to over-mix it and lose the contrast). Sprinkle the cheese on top, then place the tins under the grill or in the oven. Once the cheese has melted and begins to bubble, remove from the heat and sprinkle sesame seeds on top, 'cos burger buns have seeds… you know!

Sharing

02

Late Night Doner

Doners
450g boneless lamb shoulder,
    cut into 2cm-thick slices
450g boneless chicken thighs
600g Greek yoghurt
60ml lemon juice
150ml olive oil
2 garlic cloves, finely chopped
2 tbsp all-purpose seasoning
1 tbsp smoked paprika
2 tbsp dried mixed herbs
2 tsp fine sea salt
2 tsp cracked black pepper
1–2 large red onions, halved

Garlic Sauce
2 garlic cloves, finely chopped
100g mayo
100g natural yoghurt
grated zest of 1 unwaxed lemon
fine sea salt, to taste
cracked black pepper, to taste

Chilli Sauce
300g tinned chopped tomatoes
2 tbsp tomato ketchup
½ small onion, finely chopped
2 red chillies, seeded
2 tsp golden caster sugar
1 tsp white wine vinegar

Kebab Shop Salad
2 large cucumbers, sliced
1 iceberg lettuce, thinly sliced
4 large tomatoes, sliced
1 large onion, thinly sliced
½ red cabbage, shredded
4 whole jalapeños

To Serve
8 pitta breads

Years ago, just in front of where I live, there used be a shop called "Salamis" – salamis were the only thing they didn't sell. They made the best doner kebab in London. After it closed, I tried for years to find a doner as good as theirs; some came close, but nothing matched it. Now I just make it myself. If you like, you can get the meat marinating a day ahead, to maximise flavour, but honestly, if you don't have time, an hour will do.

MEAT
Place the slices of lamb shoulder between two sheets of clingfilm on a board and use a rolling pin to pound them and flatten them to a 1cm thickness. Transfer the lamb to a bowl. Repeat with the chicken thighs, with new sheets of clingfilm, and transfer them to a second bowl.

Combine all the remaining doner ingredients, except the onion, in a large bowl and stir well. Evenly divide the marinade between each meat bowl. Stir to coat the meat in the marinade, cover with clingfilm and pop in the fridge to marinate for at least 1 hour, ideally overnight.

SKEWER THE MEAT
Preheat oven to 190°C/Fan 170°C/Gas 5.

Place the red onion halves flat side down on a baking sheet – these will act as a base for the skewers. Push the lamb pieces onto the skewers, then push 2–3 skewers vertically into the middle of an onion half. Make sure you leave 2cm between the skewers and place them in a criss-cross formation – the criss-cross will allow them to stay balanced and to cook evenly. Repeat the same process for the chicken.

COOK
Cover the meat skewers with foil and bake for 1 hour, then take off the foil. Bake for a further 20 minutes, then remove from the oven and leave to cool for 10 minutes.

turn over

SAUCY

While the meat is resting, make the garlic sauce and chilli sauce.

For the garlic sauce, boil the kettle, then put the chopped garlic in a sieve and pour over some boiling water from the kettle – this helps tenderise the garlic. Transfer the garlic to a bowl or mortar, add a little salt and crush to form a paste. Add the remaining garlic sauce ingredients and place in a little sauce bottle if you have one (a bowl is fine if you don't).

To make the chilli sauce, pop all the ingredients into the bowl of a food-processor and blitz until smooth, then pop that into another sauce bottle or bowl.

KEBAB SHOP SALAD

Combine all the salad ingredients in a bowl and season to taste.

Now you have your own kebab shop going on. Get some pittas on the go in the toaster (on a light toast setting), maybe some chips… (no, Liam, keep this recipe relatively healthy, please). Form a pocket in a pitta, pack with meats and finish off with the salad and sauces.

TIP

If you don't like lamb, or don't like chicken, just cook one set of the skewers (halving the marinade ingredients), or double up on the meat you like.

"All the party-goers are going to come to you for that doner."

Cauliflower Show Salad

Blue Cheese Dressing
100g mayo
100g soured cream
100ml buttermilk
140g blue cheese, crumbled
2 tsp fresh lemon juice
1 tsp garlic granules

Nugget Sauce
130g gochujang (red chilli paste)
65ml dark soy sauce
3 tbsp runny honey
3 tbsp water

Cauliflower Nuggets
sunflower oil, for deep-frying
180g plain flour
1 tsp fine sea salt
1 tsp cracked black pepper
½ tsp cayenne pepper
½ tsp smoked paprika
2 large eggs
1 large cauliflower head,
　　cut into nugget-sized florets
3 tbsp sesame seeds, toasted
3 tbsp chopped chives

Salad
4 bunches of romaine
　　lettuce, chopped
4 carrots, julienned
1 large red onion, thinly sliced
150g walnuts, toasted

This recipe simply proves that you don't need meat to make a meal filling, tasty and satisfying. These little cauliflower nuggets I'm making are going to be the star of the performance, along with a couple of support acts. It's going to be a show to remember.

BLUE CHEESE DRESSING
Put the mayo, soured cream, buttermilk and 100g of the blue cheese in the bowl of a food-processor or in a blender, add the lemon juice and garlic and blitz until smooth. Transfer to a squeezy bottle or bowl and chill.

THE NUGGETS
Combine all the ingredients for the nugget sauce in a saucepan, place over a low heat and heat until it starts to simmer. Remove from the heat and keep warm.

Pour sunflower oil in the deep-fat fryer up to the safety markers and heat to 170°C. If you don't have a deep-fat fryer, use a large saucepan (filling the pan by no more than two-thirds) and a food thermometer instead. (If you don't have a thermometer, chuck a piece of cauliflower into the oil and if it bubbles and floats, the oil's ready.)

In a large bowl, whisk the flour, salt, pepper, cayenne and smoked paprika together, and in another bowl whisk the eggs. Dip some cauliflower florets into the eggs, then toss them in the flour mixture until well coated. Place on a plate and repeat with the rest of the cauliflower.

Line a large tray with kitchen paper.

DEEP-FRYING
Working in batches, fry the cauliflower nuggets in the hot oil for about 7 minutes, until golden brown. Remove the nuggets using a slotted spoon and put them on the paper-lined tray.

TOSS
Transfer the cauliflower nuggets to a large bowl, pour the nugget sauce over them, toss until well coated, then sprinkle with the sesame seeds and chives.

SALAD ASSEMBLY
Combine all the salad ingredients in a large bowl, give everything a good mix, then set aside until ready to serve.

ASSEMBLE
Place the salad on a serving dish, top the salad with the cauliflower nuggets and a generous squiggle of blue cheese dressing, then sprinkle over the remaining crumbled blue cheese.

Sharing

Sea Dogs

Crabby Patties
240g white crab meat
4 spring onions, trimmed
    and finely chopped
30g fresh coriander,
    leaves finely chopped
2 tbsp sesame seeds
100g fresh breadcrumbs
2 large egg yolks
plain flour, for dusting
2 tbsp vegetable or sunflower oil
fine sea salt, to taste
cracked black pepper, to taste

Prawns
150g raw king prawns
2 tbsp vegetable oil
1 tsp chilli powder
1 tsp smoked paprika
1 tsp garlic granules
1 tsp ground cumin
1 tsp dried mixed herbs
½ tsp freshly ground black pepper

Lime × Jalapeño Mayo
1 jalapeño, seeded
    and finely chopped
6 tbsp mayo
grated zest of 1 lime
grated zest and juice
    of 1 unwaxed lemon

To Serve
4 large hotdog buns, split in half
    lengthways and lightly toasted
½ ripe mango, peeled and
    thinly sliced
lime wedges, for squeezing

If hot dogs lived in the ocean, this is what they would look and taste like.

CRABBY PATTIES
Bung the crab, spring onions and half the coriander into a large bowl. Lightly toast the sesame seeds in a dry frying pan over a medium heat, then tip them into the bowl of crab. Add the breadcrumbs along with the egg yolks, season with salt and pepper, and give it a light mix. Shape the mixture into 12 patties, pop them on a plate and chill in the fridge for 30 minutes.

TIME TO FRY
Mix the prawns in a bowl with the oil and spices and set aside for 10 minutes.

Heat a frying pan over a medium heat, add the prawns and fry until they become pink and are cooked through, then remove them from the pan.

Lightly dust your crab patties with flour, place the frying pan back over the heat, add the oil then add half the patties and fry them gently over a medium-low heat for 3–4 minutes on each side until golden. Transfer to a plate lined with kitchen paper to absorb excess oil, then fry the remaining patties.

MAYO
Mix the jalapeño with the mayo, lime and lemon in a bowl and set to one side.

ASSEMBLE
Spread each bun with some jalapeño mayo followed by a couple of slices of mango, 3 crab patties, then some of the prawns. Drizzle over more of the jalapeño mayo and top with the remaining prawns. Sprinkle with the rest of the coriander and finish off with a cheeky squeeze of lime.

"POW! Look at that: pretty quick and super tasty!"

Sharing

The Ultimate Chippy

3 Maris Piper potatoes, peeled and
    cut into 10cm-long matchsticks
fine sea salt, to taste
cracked black pepper, to taste

Dough
500g strong white bread flour,
    plus extra for dusting
10g fast-action dried yeast
10g fine sea salt
20g golden caster sugar
40g unsalted butter, softened
340ml tepid water
oil, for greasing

Mushy Peas
500g frozen peas
50g unsalted butter
grated zest of 1 unwaxed lemon
a few mint leaves, finely
    chopped (optional)

Tartare Sauce
200g mayo
15g flat-leaf parsley, leaves picked
    and finely chopped
5g dill, leaves picked
    and finely chopped
4 tbsp baby capers,
    drained and chopped
2 pickled gherkins, chopped
juice of 1 lemon

Cod
sunflower oil, for deep-frying
200g plain flour
grated zest of 1 unwaxed lemon
1 tsp fine sea salt
1 tsp freshly ground black pepper
1 tbsp dried mixed herbs
2 large eggs, beaten
200g Panko breadcrumbs
6 pieces of cod loin (each about
    100g)

To serve
salted butter, for spreading
tomato ketchup (optional)

I hear so many people say that, at some point in their lives, their guilty pleasure has been a classic fish-finger sandwich. This is it – stepped up a bit. Imagine all the best bits from a fish and chip shop layered in simple but tasty bread rolls.

"THE BAP"
First, make the dough. Place the flour in a bowl, and put the yeast on one side and the salt, caster sugar and butter on the other. Mix to combine, then make a well in the centre and, little by little, add the water, mixing with one hand, until the ingredients come together to form a dough. Alternatively, make the dough using a stand mixer fitted with the dough hook.

Turn out the dough onto a lightly oiled surface and knead for 10 minutes, until smooth and elastic. Pop the dough in a lightly oiled bowl, cover with clingfilm or a clean tea towel and allow to rise at room temperature for 1–2 hours, or until doubled in size.

GET MUSHY WITH THOSE PEAS
While the dough is rising, make the mushy peas. Place the frozen peas in a large, heatproof bowl with 1 tablespoon of water, cover the bowl with clingfilm and heat in the microwave at full power for 2–3 minutes, until the peas are tender, then set aside to cool (alternatively, cook them in a pan of boiling water). Drain, return to the pan or bowl and blitz the peas with a stick blender, leaving a little texture (you can do this with a fork or potato masher, if you prefer).

Add the butter, lemon zest, chopped mint leaves (if using), and salt and pepper to taste. Stir to mix, then set aside.

TART UP YOUR TARTARE
Make the tartare sauce by combining all the ingredients in a bowl. Put in the fridge to chill.

SHAPE YOUR BAPS
Once the dough has doubled in size, tip it out onto a lightly oiled surface and knock it back to remove the air. Shape the dough into a ball and divide it in half.

turn over

Flatten one of the balls of dough slightly, then fold it in on itself, tucking the edges into the centre. Repeat with the other ball. Roll each ball into a narrow loaf 30–38cm long – this will give them that cool sandwich look. Transfer both to a baking tray lined with baking paper and cover with oiled clingfilm. Allow to prove at room temperature for about 1 hour, or until doubled in size.

Preheat oven to 220°C/Fan 200°C/Gas 7. Place a roasting tray at the bottom of the oven and pour boiling water into the roasting tray – this will help create the best crust on your bread.

Sprinkle your proved loaves generously with flour, then slash each loaf three times with a sharp knife. Bake for 35–40 minutes, until risen and golden brown and the bases sound hollow when tapped. Remove from the oven and leave to cool on the tray until you're ready to assemble the sarnie.

FISH AND CHIP TIME
Pour sunflower oil in the deep-fat fryer up to the safety markers and heat to 170°C. If you don't have a deep-fat fryer, use a large saucepan and a cooking thermometer instead (filling the pan by no more than two-thirds).

Make the coating for the fish. Place three plates with lips, or wide, shallow bowls, on the surface. Combine the flour, lemon zest, salt, pepper and mixed herbs in one. Pour the beaten egg into another, and evenly spread the Panko breadcrumbs on the third.

Completely coat each cod loin piece in the flour mixture, then the egg, then the breadcrumbs. Fry the loin pieces in the fryer basket of the deep-fat fryer for 2 minutes, until golden brown on the outside and flaky in the middle. (You may need to do this in batches, 2 pieces at a time, to avoid them sticking together or cooling down the oil too much.) Transfer the cooked fish to a plate lined with kitchen paper and keep warm.

Make the fries. Place a small handful of the chips into the fryer basket in the oil and fry for 1 minute, until golden brown – watch carefully or else they will burn. Remove the basket from the fryer and allow the chips to drain in the basket, then transfer to a bowl lined with kitchen paper and sprinkle with salt. Repeat with the remaining chips until all the fries are cooked.

SANDWICH ASSEMBLY
To assemble the sarnie, cut the loaves in half lengthways along their middles and spread one half of each loaf with some salted butter. Place generous dollops of the mushy peas along the base and spread out evenly. Pop the breaded cod loin on top of the peas, then slather over the tartare sauce. Top with the fries and finish off with the top half of the loaves.

Cut each sandwich into 3 or 4 portions to share with your pals. If you have ketchup – you know what to do. Ketchup makes everything better.

Prawn × Waffles

Curried Prawns
375g pumpkin or butternut squash,
    peeled and cut into 2cm chunks
375g potatoes, peeled and
    cut into 2cm chunks
4 tbsp vegetable oil
1 large onion, finely chopped
3 garlic cloves, finely chopped
10cm piece fresh root ginger,
    peeled and grated
2 large green peppers,
    seeded and chopped
4 tsp mild curry powder
1 tsp ground turmeric
1 tsp garam masala
1 tsp ground coriander
2 tsp all-purpose seasoning
1 Scotch bonnet chilli
3 x 200g bags peeled,
    raw prawns (thawed if frozen)
fine sea salt, to taste
cracked black pepper, to taste

Savoury Waffles
3 large eggs
450ml whole milk
340g self-raising flour
3 tsp baking powder
1 tsp smoked paprika
1 tsp cracked black pepper
1 tsp fine sea salt
225g unsalted butter, melted
    and cooled, plus a little
    extra for frying
25g fresh chives

To Serve
fresh coriander
mango chutney

Honestly, I don't know where the waffle element in this recipe came from but I sure do know where the prawns came from: the sea. Ha! "Sea" what I done there. My nan is known to many as the queen and king of Caribbean curries. You had the nan-inspired curry goat recipe, now behold the prawn curry, again packed with a silly amount of flavour, little tender chunks of pumpkin and not-so-sweet potatoes. All served on some super crisp waffles – no machine needed! Madness.

STEAM
Bring a large saucepan of water to the boil and place a steam basket over it. Add the pumpkin and potatoes to the basket, cover with a lid and steam for 20 minutes or until they are almost tender.

CURRY
Heat the vegetable oil in a large frying pan over a medium heat, add the onion, garlic, ginger and green peppers and fry gently for 6–7 minutes until the onions and peppers are soft and tender.

Take the steamer basket off the saucepan, reserve a large cupful of the water from the saucepan and pour away the excess. Put the pumpkin and potato in the saucepan along with the fried onions and pepper mixture, and add the spices and half of the water. Place over a medium-low heat and simmer for 10–15 minutes until the pumpkin and potato are completely tender and the sauce is thick (you might need to add the rest of the water if it gets too thick). Season to taste with salt and pepper.

Cut a few slits in the Scotch bonnet chilli with a knife. Turn up the heat, drop the chilli and prawns into the pan and stir well. Once the curry starts to boil, reduce the heat again and cook the prawns for 10–15 minutes until they turn pink and are cooked through. The curry should be thick and super tasty. Remove from the heat and cover to keep warm while you make the waffles (remove the Scotch bonnet at this point, if you like).

THE WAFFLES
Crack the eggs into a large bowl, add the milk and whisk. Sift the flour, baking powder and smoked paprika, add them to the bowl with the pepper and salt and whisk again until well incorporated. Next, add the cool melted butter to the batter, snip in the chives and stir.

turn over

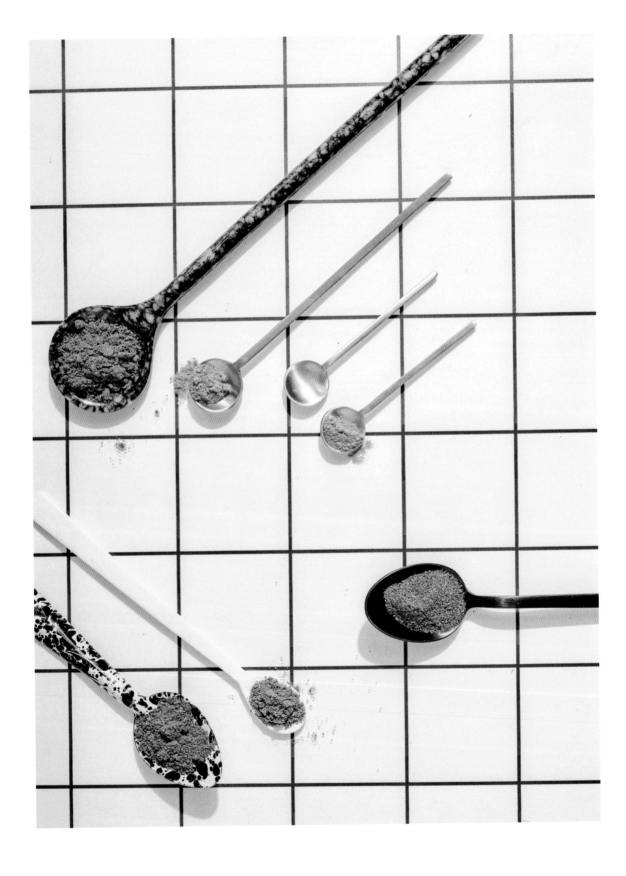

Pop a griddle pan over a high heat and add a little extra butter. Once it's melted, pour in some of the waffle batter and spread it around to fill the pan. Turn the heat down to medium and cook for 5–6 minutes or until a light golden brown on the bottom. Give it a cheeky flip and cook for a further 6 minutes. Transfer to a plate and repeat with the remaining batter until all the mixture is used (you should have enough mixture to make 6–8 waffles).

"I tell you what. For extra crispness, give each side another minute if you fancy."

ASSEMBLE
Pour the prawn curry into a large serving bowl, cut the savoury waffles into triangles and place them around the bowl. Sprinkle with fresh coriander and serve with mango chutney on the side.

"Go on. I'm not dishing up — help yourself. All you need is a spoon each: grab a waffle, top with a couple of spoonfuls of curry, and maybe a little mango chutney. Sorted."

Sharing

Duck Rotitos

Serves 4 — Skill Level: you got this

Quack
- a large bunch of spring onions, trimmed and roughly chopped
- 10cm piece fresh root ginger, peeled and roughly chopped
- 1 small onion, roughly chopped
- 1 Scotch bonnet chilli
- 2 tbsp dried mixed herbs
- juice of 1 lime
- 3 tbsp dark soy sauce
- 2 tbsp vegetable oil
- 4 tbsp soft dark brown sugar
- 1½ tbsp ground allspice
- 4 large duck breasts

Rice × Peas
- 3 tbsp olive oil
- ½ onion, roughly chopped
- 1 red pepper, seeded and chopped
- 1 green pepper, seeded and chopped
- 2 garlic cloves, finely chopped
- 2 sprigs of thyme
- 2 tsp ground allspice
- 1 vegetable stock cube
- 200g long-grain rice
- 200ml water
- 200ml coconut milk
- 1 x 400g tin kidney beans, drained and rinsed
- a small bunch of coriander, leaves chopped
- fine sea salt, to taste
- cracked black pepper, to taste

Jerk-hacked Plum × Hoisin Sauce
- 300g soured cream
- 50ml plum sauce
- 50ml hoisin sauce
- 2 tsp ground allspice
- ¼ tsp freshly grated nutmeg
- 2 tbsp chilli sauce

Simple Salad
- ½ large iceberg lettuce, roughly chopped
- 2 large tomatoes, diced
- 1 x 198g tin sweetcorn, drained (or 165g frozen sweetcorn)
- 1 red onion, sliced

Sometimes I feel like eating some good Mexican food, but other times – especially on a Saturday – you'll catch me at my favourite Caribbean restaurant in Stoke Newington eating a roti. What if I want both? Fear not, this is the recipe. Get someone else to help you make them: you can get a little system going with the prep and assembling of the roti wraps.

QUACK
Put all the ingredients for the duck (other than the breasts themselves) in the bowl of a food-processor and blitz to form a smooth paste.

Score the skin of the duck breasts with a sharp knife in a criss-cross pattern. Rub the jerk paste over the duck breasts and leave to sit at room temperature for at least 1 hour.

RICE × PEAS
Heat the olive oil in a saucepan, add the veg and fry for 2–3 minutes, then add the garlic, spices, stock cube (crumbled in) and some salt and pepper. Cook over a medium-low heat for about 10 minutes until softened. Meanwhile, rinse and rub the rice in a few changes of cold water, until the water is clear, not cloudy.

Add the rice, water and coconut milk to the pan of vegetables and bring to the boil. Pop in the kidney beans, stir, cover, reduce the heat to low and simmer gently for 20 minutes, or until the rice is cooked and all the water and coconut milk has been absorbed. Season to taste with a little salt and pepper and turn off the heat. Remove the thyme sprigs, cover and set aside, sprinkled with the coriander, until ready to serve.

PAN-FRY QUACK
Preheat oven to 200°C/Fan 180°C/Gas 6.

Place the duck breasts skin side down in a large frying pan with no oil and place on the hob over a low heat (or cook them in batches of two at a time in a smaller pan). Cook for 8 minutes, gradually increasing the heat, until the skin is golden brown, then flip the duck breasts over and lightly brown the other side. The breasts should feel slightly springy to the touch (a bit like a cake... okay,

turn over for more ingredients

Sharing

69

To Serve
4 roti wrap skins
a large handful
  of plantain chips

maybe not). Transfer to a baking dish (or keep them in the frying pan if your pan is ovenproof) and roast in the oven for a further 10 minutes. Remove, transfer to a plate, cover with foil and let the duck rest while you crack on with the other stuff.

SAUCE × SIMPLE SALAD
Combine all the ingredients for the sauce and all the ingredients for the salad (in separate bowls) and keep in the fridge until ready to serve.

ASSEMBLE
Slice the duck breasts. Heat each roti skin in a frying pan for 15–30 seconds, until warmed through. Place the roti skins on a surface and pile a quarter of the rice into the centre of each wrap. Top with some salad, followed by sliced duck breast and, finally, dollops of the good, good sauce. Fold one edge over the filling, then fold in the remaining sides, like an envelope. Serve the wraps with plantain chips.

"This one is probs one of my faves. Shhh… Don't tell my other recipes that."

TIP
For the best flavour experience use roti skins, but if you can't find them (the best ones can be found in Tottenham, by the way), use large flour tortilla wraps. They will work almost just as well.

Pancake Tacos

Pancake Taco Shells
220g plain flour
1 tbsp baking powder
4 tbsp light muscovado sugar
1½ tsp fine sea salt
1 large egg
300ml whole milk
2 tsp vanilla extract or vanilla
    bean paste
2 tbsp melted unsalted butter
vegetable or sunflower oil,
    for frying the pancakes

Salsa
4 large tomatoes, diced
2 red onions, finely chopped
1 garlic clove, crushed
juice of 1 lime
a small bunch of coriander,
    roughly chopped
fine sea salt, to taste
cracked black pepper, to taste

Scrambled Eggs
12 large eggs
30g unsalted butter
60ml whole milk

Add-ons
12 rashers unsmoked bacon
2 ripe avocados, peeled
    and thinly sliced
5 tbsp maple syrup
300g thinly sliced smoked
    salmon
80g pesto

Give the humble taco shell a rest just for this recipe – I swear
it will be back later – and replace it with the fluffiest of pancakes,
which here encase the champions of breakfast: scrambled eggs
and bacon or smoked salmon (knowing Babs, he will probably
have both), a couple of slices of avocado, and a salsa of all salsas.
It's no cutlery, no fuss and every pancake gets a bit of loving
from the filling, not just the top one (selfish top pancake, lol).
Oi! Making breakfast recipes is mad fun you know!

PANCAKE TACOS
Pop the flour, baking powder, sugar and salt in a large bowl and
make a well in the middle. In a separate jug beat the egg with
the milk, vanilla extract and melted butter. Beating with a whisk,
gradually add the wet ingredients to the dry ingredients until
well combined.

Add a couple of squiggles of oil to a large frying pan then give the
pan a wipe with kitchen paper. Place the pan over a medium heat.

Cook your pancakes in the greased frying pan one at a time,
using about 60ml batter (¼ cup portions) for each pancake. Flip
the pancake after a couple of minutes – the edges should be dry
and you should be able to see bubbles form on top and gradually
burst. Now flip the pancake over and cook on the other side for
a further 2 minutes. Don't forget to re-grease the pan with oil each
time. Keep the cooked pancakes warm while you cook the rest
(the mixture should make 12 pancakes).

SALSA
Combine all the salsa ingredients in a bowl, give everything a good
stir and store in the fridge until ready to serve.

BACON
Add the bacon rashers to the frying pan you cooked the pancakes
in and cook over a medium heat for about 8 minutes, then flip
them over and cook until well crisped on both sides. Remove from
the heat and place on kitchen paper to drain excess fat.

SCRAMBLING
Crack the eggs into the measuring jug and give them a quick beat
with a fork.

Sharing

turn over

Put a medium saucepan or frying pan over a low heat, add the butter and milk, allow the butter to melt, then add the eggs and very slowly begin to stir with a spatula or a wooden spoon.

There are times where your eggs may look a little scary but continue to stir until the eggs are looking slightly runny and undercooked. Remove the pan from the heat. Continue to stir while it's off the heat: the pan will continue to cook the eggs – residual heat, init.

"I will never let you eat raw scrambled egg, trust me."

TACOS ASSEMBLY

Fold one pancake into a taco shape and prop it up between two cups or glasses (if you have a taco holder that would be awesome).

Place some of the scrambled egg into the taco, slot 2 bacon rashers between the egg and the pancake, top with a few avocado slices and some salsa. Drizzle with a little maple syrup. For the fish pancake taco, swap the bacon for smoked salmon, and instead of the maple syrup go for the pesto. Repeat with the remaining pancakes.

"Make these on the fly: if you fancy another one, go ahead, don't be shy!"

TIP

Go mental and express your "taconess" with different fillings. Try adding a sausage to the mix instead of bacon.

Pick It × Dip It × Wing It

Wings
16 jumbo chicken wings
200g plain flour
3 tsp cracked black pepper
4 tbsp all-purpose seasoning
2 tsp fine sea salt

Curly Fries
4 large potatoes, peeled
1 tsp smoked paprika
½ tsp ground cumin
1 tsp garlic granules
1 tsp mild chilli powder
1 tsp fine sea salt
1 tsp cracked black pepper
4 tbsp vegetable oil

The Sauces

BBQ Belters
150g BBQ sauce
85g runny honey
1 tsp smoked paprika
1 tsp garlic granules

Buffalo
150ml hot sauce (I like Dunn's
    River Jamaican hot sauce)
10ml red wine vinegar
1 tbsp Worcestershire sauce
½ tsp fine sea salt
½ tsp garlic granules
100g unsalted butter

Lemon × Herb
4 tbsp olive oil
2 garlic cloves, crushed
4 tbsp dried mixed herbs
1 tbsp chopped fresh flat-leaf parsley
fine sea salt, to taste
1 tsp finely ground black pepper
juice of 1 lemon

Fishy Caramel
60ml fish sauce
60g caster sugar
3 garlic cloves, crushed
a small bunch of coriander,
    leaves chopped

To Serve
blue cheese sauce
peri peri sauce
tomato ketchup
mustard of choice

If you ever go out with me, to any restaurant, food market, or even to a vegan place, I'm always asking for CHICKEN WINGS. I love them: fried, baked, grilled, steamed, boiled (um, dunno about boiled), with all different types of sauces. If I'm perfectly honest, chicken wings are the best way to determine just how good a food place is. They're so easy to make perfectly, but also so simple to mess up. This recipe is all about appreciation of chicken wings, with a few extra trimmings, of course.

BAKE WINGS × FRIES
Preheat oven to 200°C/Fan 180°C/Gas 6 and line two baking trays with baking paper.

Combine all the dry ingredients for the wings in a large bowl, then lightly toss each wing in the mixture before placing it on the lined baking trays. Bake for 40 minutes, turning the wings over halfway through cooking, until the skin is crispy and golden brown.

Spiralize the potatoes using a spiralizer (if you don't have one, just cut the potatoes into thin chips). Lay the fries flat on a baking tray, add the spices, salt and pepper and the oil and give it a good mix with your hands. Bake for 25–30 minutes, until crisp, turning them occasionally, then remove from the oven and set aside to cool.

STEEPED IN SAUCE
While the fries and wings bake, crack on with your sauces. For all four sauces, it's the same principle: combine all the ingredients for that specific sauce in a pan, place over a medium heat and cook for a couple of minutes. Make one sauce at a time.

Place each cooked sauce in a separate heatproof bowl. Divide the wings into four portions of four and toss each portion in a separate bowl, until each wing is well coated in sauce, then return all the wings back to the baking trays and bake for a further 6–10 minutes.

ASSEMBLE
Place all the wings on a large serving platter, with the curly fries on the side. Place the blue cheese sauce, peri peri sauce, ketchup and mustard directly in the centre.

Now the only thing to do is pick, dip and wing it.

Rudolph Dogs

4 large turkey sausages
4 large, soft hot-dog rolls
unsalted butter, for spreading
fine sea salt, to taste
cracked black pepper, to taste

Chestnut Stuffing Crumb
3 tbsp sunflower oil
1 large onion, diced
1 garlic clove, finely chopped
150g wild mushrooms, chopped
45g salted butter
2 tbsp dried mixed herbs
90g vacuum-packed
    cooked chestnuts
50g stale wholemeal breadcrumbs
a small bunch of parsley,
    leaves picked
2 sprigs of thyme, leaves picked

Cranberry Sauce
2 tbsp cornflour
4 tbsp cold water
375g frozen cranberries
grated zest of 1 orange
150ml fresh orange juice
150ml soft light brown sugar
1 tbsp peeled and freshly
    grated root ginger
1 cinnamon stick

Cheese × Chive Mayo
110g mayo
65g mature Cheddar, grated
2 tsp dried mixed herbs
½ tsp English mustard powder
½ tsp garlic granules
3 tbsp snipped fresh chives, plus
extra to garnish

Christmas is one of my favourite times of the year, mainly because of the amount of food there is to eat. With a couple of Christmassy twists here and there, you might be persuaded to rustle these up on Christmas Eve.

STUFFING CRUMB

Preheat oven to 190°C/Fan 170°C/Gas 5. Heat the oil in a frying pan over a medium heat, add the onion, garlic and mushrooms and cook for 6 minutes, until the vegetables start to soften.

Pop the softened onion, garlic and mushrooms into the bowl of a food-processor along with the remaining stuffing ingredients, season with salt and pepper and blitz until the mixture is just about coming together.

Spread the mixture out on a baking tray and bake for about 40 minutes, turning and stirring the mixture halfway through, until crispy. Remove from the oven and allow to cool.

GOBBLE GOBBLE

While the stuffing is cooking, crack on with everything else. Heat a little sunflower oil in a frying pan over a medium heat, add the turkey sausages and fry for 8–10 minutes, or until they are well cooked through. Remove from the heat and put on a plate until you're ready to serve.

CRANBERRY SAUCE

Combine the cornflour with the water. Tip the frozen cranberries into a saucepan, add the cornflour mixture, orange zest and juice, sugar, ginger and cinnamon. Place over a medium heat and simmer for 5–10 minutes, until they are softened but still hold their shape. Remove from the heat and leave the sauce to cool – it will thicken up, trust me – then place in the fridge until ready to use.

CHEESE MAYO × ASSEMBLE

Pop all the mayo ingredients, except the chives, in the bowl of a food-processor and blitz until smooth, then stir through the chives to combine.

Slice all the rolls in half lengthways and spread them with a generous amount of butter.

Heat a frying pan over a medium heat. Once hot, pop the rolls face down in the pan for 30 seconds–1 minute, until golden brown. Place a turkey sausage in each toasted bun, top with cranberry sauce, a couple of clusters of the stuffing and squiggles of the cheese and chive mayo. Sprinkle with some chives and serve.

Sharing

Bao Bao Fire Buns

Buns
500g plain flour
40g caster sugar
1 tsp smoked paprika
½ tsp ground cinnamon
1 tsp baking powder
1 tsp fine sea salt
10g fast-action dried yeast
150ml lukewarm water
150ml lukewarm whole milk

Sticky Pork
700g boneless pork shoulder,
    thinly sliced
1 onion, thinly sliced
3 spring onions, trimmed
    and thinly sliced
3 garlic cloves, crushed
60g gochujang (red chilli paste)
1 tsp dried chilli flakes
70ml light soy sauce
2 tbsp rice wine
2 tbsp sesame oil
1 tbsp golden caster sugar
1 tsp ground black pepper
2 tbsp vegetable oil, plus
    extra for greasing

Mayo
100g mayo
2 tsp wasabi paste
grated zest and juice of 1 lime

To Finish
sesame seeds
2 spring onions, trimmed
    and thinly sliced
a handful of prawn crackers,
    roughly broken

Give me any bao bun, any time, any place, I'm there. I've eaten so many of them recently, from sausage or salmon to BBQ beef buns, honestly I don't know of anything you could put between those pillowy bun lips that could taste wrong. For this number, I've gone for a traditional filling of pork, with sticky Korean sauce. And the mayooooooooo. Don't get me started...

BUNS I
Stir all the dry ingredients for the buns together in a bowl, but add the salt and yeast last and make sure the salt doesn't come in direct contact with the yeast. Using a stand mixer fitted with a dough hook (or your hands), gradually add the water and milk, mixing until the mixture forms a dough. Knead for 10 minutes (on a lightly oiled work surface if kneading by hand), or until the dough is smooth and no longer sticky.

Form the dough into a ball with a little oil on your hands. Place the dough in a lightly oiled bowl, cover with clingfilm and leave to prove at room temperature for 1 hour, or until doubled in size.

THE FILLING
While the dough is proving, make the filling. Put the pork and the rest of the filling ingredients, except the oil, in a bowl and mix with your hands until the pork is well coated. Cover with clingfilm and pop in the fridge for 30 minutes.

MAYO
Combine all the ingredients in a bowl and store in the fridge until ready to serve.

BUNS II
Knock back the bun dough and roll the dough into a sausage shape about 4cm wide and 30cm long. Divide it into 10 equal portions (roughly 70–75g each). Roll each portion into a ball, then flatten them with the palm of your hand into 3–4mm-thick ovals.

Rub a little oil on each oval then place a chopstick or skewer in the middle of each oval. Fold the dough over the chopstick or skewer, place on a baking tray lined with baking paper and loosely cover with oiled clingfilm. Allow to prove at room temperature for a further 30 minutes.

turn over

Sharing

COOK THE PORK

Heat the vegetable oil in a large frying pan over a high heat. Add some of the pork (cook it in batches) and stir-fry it for 5 minutes until slightly crispy around the edges and cooked through. Transfer to a heatproof dish and cook the remaining pork. Keep the pork warm while you steam the buns.

STEAM

Bring some water to a simmer in a medium saucepan, pop a bamboo steamer or a metal steamer basket with a lid on top of the pan (make sure the water doesn't touch the steamer) and line it with baking paper. Remove the chopsticks or skewers from the buns then steam them (in batches if necessary) over a medium heat for 20 minutes until puffed up. Turn off the heat and leave them in the steamer for 5 minutes, then remove and allow to cool to room temperature.

ASSEMBLE

Split the buns open and generously stuff each bao bun with the pork, along with a drizzle of mayo, a sprinkle of sesame seeds and sliced spring onions, and a couple of pieces of prawn cracker.

"They're not called 'fire buns' because of the spice level, it's solely because of the flavours. They are powerful."

Chicken Katsu Doughnut

Sharing

vegetable oil, for deep-frying
fine sea salt, to taste
cracked black pepper, to taste

Doughnut Dough
500g strong white bread flour,
    plus extra for dusting
2 tsp ground turmeric
2 tsp mild curry powder
1 tsp dried chilli flakes
50g caster sugar
10g fine sea salt
15g fresh yeast (or 8g fast-action
    dried yeast)
75ml water, at room temperature
75ml whole milk,
    at room temperature
4 large eggs
2 tbsp dark soy sauce
125g unsalted butter, softened

Katsu Nutty Chicken
5 large chicken breasts,
    skin removed
300ml buttermilk
2 tsp smoked paprika, or to taste
2 tbsp light soy sauce, or to taste
3 tbsp hoisin sauce, or to taste

Chicken Coating
200g tortilla chips, crushed
300g Panko breadcrumbs
200g roasted cashew nuts,
    blitzed to coarse crumbs
100g plain flour
4 large eggs, beaten

Pickled Slaw
4 carrots, julienned
½ red cabbage, cored
    and thinly sliced
½ cucumber, seeded and
    cut into thin batons
1 red onion, thinly sliced
leaves from a couple
    of coriander sprigs, chopped
a big handful of beansprouts
2 tbsp runny honey
½ tbsp sesame oil
4 tbsp apple cider vinegar
1 tsp fine sea salt

Chicken katsu has taken the food scene by storm recently, whether that's in a burger bun, served with rice, noodles, salad or just by itself. But wait... what if it was served in a savoury doughnut alongside pickled slaw and Japanese-hacked mayo? Sounds wicked, init!

DAY I

DOUGH I

Start by making the dough. Put all of the dough ingredients, apart from the butter, into the bowl of a stand mixer fitted with the beater attachment, crumbling in the yeast. Mix on medium speed for 10 minutes, or until the dough forms a ball and comes away from the sides of the bowl.

Leave the dough to rest for 5 minutes.

Slowly add the butter to the dough, about 25g at a time, with the beater back on medium speed. Once all the butter is incorporated, increase the speed to high and mix for 5–7 minutes until the dough is glossy and super elastic.

Cover the bowl with clingfilm and leave the dough to prove at room temperature for 2–3 hours, or until it has doubled in size.

Once it has doubled in size, tip it out onto a lightly floured surface, knock it back, then return it to the bowl. Cover with clingfilm again and put in the fridge to chill overnight and double in size.

KATSU NUTTY CHICKEN

While the dough is having its first prove, prepare the chicken. Put the chicken breasts in a bowl and pour over the buttermilk. Add the smoked paprika, soy sauce and hoisin sauce. Season with salt and pepper. Give the chicken a good rub, cover the bowl with clingfilm and marinate in the fridge overnight.

DAY II

DOUGH II

Tip the risen dough out onto a lightly floured surface and knock it back. Divide it into 10 pieces, each weighing about 50g, then roll each piece into a ball. Cut out 10 squares of baking paper measuring 10 x 10cm. Place each dough ball onto a square of

turn over for more ingredients

Katsu Mayo
300g mayo
3 tbsp hoisin sauce
2 tsp medium curry powder
1 tsp garam masala
¼ tsp ground cloves
juice of ½ lime
2 tsp five-spice powder

paper and lightly dust the dough balls with flour. Cover with clingfilm and leave to rise at room temperature for about 1 hour until doubled in size.

PICKLED SLAW
Combine the carrot, cabbage, cucumber, red onion, coriander and beansprouts in a bowl. Whisk the honey, sesame oil and vinegar with the salt in a separate, large bowl. Add the combined veg to the bowl, give it a good toss and set aside.

KATSU MAYO
To make the katsu mayo, combine all the ingredients in a bowl and chill until needed. You can put a couple of tablespoons of the mayo into the slaw if you wish.

FRY THE CHICKEN
Take the chicken out of the fridge and allow it to come up to room temperature.

For the coating, combine the crushed tortilla chips, breadcrumbs and cashews in a large, wide bowl. Put the flour into another large bowl, and the beaten eggs in another.

Pour vegetable oil in the deep-fat fryer up to the safety markers and heat to 180°C. If you don't have a deep-fat fryer, use a large saucepan and a cooking thermometer instead (filling the pan by no more than two-thirds). Line a baking tray with kitchen paper.

Remove the excess buttermilk from each chicken breast. One by one, roll each chicken breast in the flour, then the egg and finally in the breadcrumb mixture.

Deep-fry the coated chicken breasts in batches for 1 minute 30 seconds–2 minutes on each side, until the chicken is cooked through (about 75°C on a probe thermometer) and the coating is crisp and golden brown. Transfer each batch of chicken to the tray lined with kitchen paper, to soak up excess oil. Cut each breast in half (to give you 10 pieces) and set aside to keep warm.

FRY THE DOUGHNUTS
Line another baking tray with kitchen paper. Using the same oil in the deep-fat fryer at 180°C, carefully put 2 or 3 of the risen doughnuts in the fryer at a time (if the paper sticks, don't worry – just remove it carefully with tongs when it comes free in the oil). Fry the doughnuts for 2 minutes on each side – flipping them with metal tongs or two wooden skewers – until golden, then drain on the paper-lined tray. Repeat for all the doughnuts.

Take one doughnut at a time and cut it in half. Top one half with a little pickled slaw, then a piece of chicken and a good dollop of mayo. Finish off with the other half of the doughnut and use a skewer to hold it all in place. Repeat for all the chicken pieces, slaw, mayo and doughnuts and serve immediately.

Kofta Focaccia

Focaccia Dough
450g strong white bread flour
50g fine semolina
½ tsp fine sea salt
310ml lukewarm water
1 tbsp golden caster sugar
10g fast-action dried yeast
olive oil, for greasing

Lamb Kofta
750g lamb mince
4 tsp ground cumin
5 tsp ground coriander
2 tbsp chopped fresh mint leaves
2 large garlic cloves, crushed
olive oil, for brushing
fine sea salt, to taste
cracked black pepper, to taste

Focaccia Topping
2 tbsp olive oil
2 red onions, thinly sliced
3 sprigs of thyme, leaves picked
5 tbsp balsamic vinegar
a small handful of rosemary,
    needles picked

Garlic Sauce
300g Greek yoghurt
2 garlic cloves, crushed
2 tbsp finely chopped fresh mint
grated zest and juice of
    1 unwaxed lemon
3 tsp capers, drained
    and roughly chopped

Special Salad
1 large red onion, halved
    and thinly sliced
2 tsp sumac
2 tsp dried chilli flakes
3 large tomatoes, quartered
a bunch of flat-leaf parsley,
    roughly chopped
juice of 1 lemon
1 tbsp extra virgin olive oil

To Serve
hummus
olive oil

The best part of a Turkish meal are those grilled meats, especially the lamb kofta and that warm, soft bread. I swear if I didn't have self-control I would gladly eat the whole lot, so a recipe that combines the two, with a couple of add-ons, has to be a winner!

FOCACCIA DOUGH
Put the flour, semolina and salt in a large bowl and use your hands to make a well in the middle. Put the water in a jug or bowl, add the sugar and yeast and mix with a spoon. Gradually pour the liquid into the well, mixing with a fork as you go. Once it comes together, knead for 5 minutes until the dough is smooth, soft, and springs back when you press it. Lightly grease a large bowl with oil, pop your dough into the bowl, cover with a tea towel and allow to prove at room temperature for 30 minutes–1 hour until it has doubled in size.

KOFTAS × ONIONS
While the dough is proving, move on to the koftas. Mix all the ingredients together in a bowl until well combined and season with salt and pepper. Split evenly into 12 balls, then shape each ball into an oval.

Heat a griddle pan over a medium heat and brush it with olive oil. Add the koftas and cook them on each side for 3 minutes. It will be very tempting, but resist turning the koftas over until the meat is well browned because otherwise the meat will stick to the pan, and that's sad. Remove from the heat and transfer to a plate.

Heat the olive oil for the focaccia topping in a frying pan over a low heat. Add the onions and thyme leaves and fry for 5 minutes, then add the balsamic vinegar and cook for another couple of minutes until syrupy. Remove from the heat and set aside to cool.

GARLIC SAUCE × SALAD
Combine all the garlic sauce ingredients in a bowl, then pop in the fridge until ready to use.

To make the salad, put the red onion in a large bowl, add the sumac and give it a good rub with your hands. This will infuse the onion with the spice as well as softening it.

turn over

Sharing

Add all the remaining salad ingredients to the bowl of onions, stir and season with salt and pepper. Cover and put in the fridge until ready to serve.

BAKE
Preheat oven to 220°C/Fan 200°C/Gas 7 and line the baking tray with baking paper.

Once the dough has risen, knock it back, then place it on the lined baking tray and gently spread it out to cover the tray. Now poke little holes and dips all over the dough using your fingers.

"A lot of typing on the computer for practice should help."

Spread the onion and thyme topping over the surface of the focaccia. Roughly chop the kofta into large chunks and add them to the surface. Lastly, dot the rosemary all around the focaccia. Prove at room temperature, covered with a clean tea towel or clingfilm, for another 15 minutes then bake for 20 minutes. It should super soft in the middle and golden around the edges.

Remove the focaccia from the oven.

ASSEMBLE
This is the best part. Once the focaccia has slightly cooled, spread the salad over the top and drop generous dollops of the yoghurt sauce over it. If you have any hummus and oil lying around, you know what to do.

Quick Fix

03

Halloooumi Chips × Dip

Harissa Yoghurt Swirl
200g Greek yoghurt
grated zest of 1 unwaxed lemon,
    lemon then cut into wedges
2 tbsp runny honey
3 tbsp rose harissa
a handful of mint

Halloumi
2 x 250g blocks halloumi,
    cut into fat chunks
2 tbsp za'atar or dried
    mixed herbs
100g plain flour
500ml–1 litre sunflower
    oil, for deep-frying

I don't know anyone who doesn't like halloumi, unless you have a dairy intolerance (but even saying that, you would still take one for the team if you had to). These chips are ridiculously versatile, so you can put pretty much anything with them and it will only complement the saltiness of the cheese. OOOOO, and another thing, they go down really well at parties!

HARISSA SWIRLY YOGHURT
Mix the yoghurt in a bowl with the lemon zest and honey. Swirl the rose harissa into the yoghurt.

"Doing this allows you to have hot, cool, but sweet vibes going on."

HALLOUMI
Preheat oven to 160°C/Fan 140°C/Gas 3.

Pat the halloumi chunks with kitchen paper. Put the za'atar or herbs and plain flour on a plate and stir to combine. Coat the halloumi chips in the flour mixture.

Heat a heavy, deep pan two-thirds filled with sunflower oil until it reaches 180°C. Now, working in small batches, lower the chips into the oil and cook for 2–4 minutes until crisp and golden brown, then drain on kitchen paper.

These fries are at their best when they're warm, so once you've fried them, pop them in the warm oven on a baking tray until ready to eat.

Serve with the lemon wedges and the yoghurt dip.

"Remember, these are best served warm, so make 'em quick and eat 'em quick, of course."

Quick Fix

Serves 4
Skill Level: **light work**

4 large apples (any type will work),
    peeled, cored and chopped
200g fresh blackberries
600g Greek yoghurt
1 tsp ground cinnamon
1 tsp ground cardamom
1 tsp freshly grated nutmeg
430ml unsweetened almond milk
2 tbsp runny honey

To Finish
thinly sliced apple
50g fresh blackberries
your favourite granola, for sprinkling

Apple × Blackberry Crumble Smoothie

I don't know how many recipe books I will write in my lifetime, but for every book I write there will always be an apple-crumble-inspired something. In my last book there was a layer cake and tart, this time it's a smoothie, baby! Let's gooooo!

HEALTHY CRUMBLE
Put all the ingredients in a blender and blitz until smooth. Pour the smoothie into glasses or jars and top each portion with thinly sliced apple, blackberries and a generous sprinkle of granola.

Serves 4
Skill Level: **light work**

400g natural yoghurt
100ml whole milk
1 large banana, chopped and frozen
400g frozen mixed berries
2 x 27g sachets of quick oats
3 tbsp runny honey
1 tbsp flaxseeds
handful of ice cubes

To Serve
200g natural yoghurt
your favourite granola, for sprinkling

Biggy Brekky Smoothie

This pretty much does what it says on the label: it's tasty, satisfying breakfast in a cup, full of slow-energy-releasing ingredients. You'll be tempted to go back for more, but maybe save yourself, because you have lunch, dinner and (of course) dessert. If you are short for time in the mornings, this is the brekky for you.

WHIZZ × SHIZZ
Pop all the ingredients in a blender and blitz at high speed until smooth. Pour into four cups. Top with a dollop of yoghurt and a light sprinkling of granola.

Serves 2
Skill Level: **light work**

500ml unsweetened almond milk
2 large bananas, chopped and frozen
6 Medjool dates, stoned
4 tbsp runny honey
4 tbsp smooth peanut butter
½ tsp ground cinnamon,
    plus extra to serve
a handful of ice cubes

Smooooooooth Talker

I would not consider myself to be a smooth talker. My smoothies do a far better job, because once you have a slurp, shhh, do you hear that?… silence! Told you this smoothie is a smooth talker.

WHIZZ × SHIZZ
Pop all the ingredients in a blender and blitz at high speed until smooth. Pour into two cups and serve, topped with a light sprinkle of ground cinnamon.

The "Glow Up" Smoothie

Serves 4
Skill Level: light work

250ml unsweetened almond milk,
    plus extra to serve (if needed)
2 medium bananas, peeled
2 handfuls of spinach, washed
1 ripe avocado, peeled and diced
400g fresh blueberries
2 tbsp cashew butter
2 tbsp ground flaxseed
½ tsp ground cinnamon
2 handfuls of ice cubes (optional)

It's fair to say you can find avocados in almost everything. It's a brilliant alternative to conventional dairy ingredients because it has a smooth, creamy consistency similar to butter, milk and ice cream. Oh, and don't get me started on the health benefits. All I can say is that this will help you "glow up".

TIME TO GLOW
Pop all the ingredients in a blender and blitz until smooth. If you fancy a thick smoothie, add the ice cubes before blitzing, but if you want it to be slightly thinner, and to be shared with more people, add a couple splashes of almond milk.

Vibey

Serves 4
Skill Level: light work

250g diced mango
    (from 1–2 mangoes)
250g diced peach
    (from 4–5 peaches)
150g diced pineapple
200g Greek yoghurt
200ml whole milk
1 tbsp chia seeds
1 tsp peeled and grated
    fresh root ginger
½ tsp ground turmeric
2 ice cubes

Everyone loves a good smoothie, especially when it has summer vibes. We're talking mangoes, peaches, a little pineapple, then – to combat the sweetness – there's ginger and yes, we said it, turmeric. I tell you what, whip this one up on a sunny day, give a glass of it to your neighbour and I can promise you you'll be best friends and borrowing their lawnmower before you know it.

GOOD VIBES
Put all the ingredients in a blender and blitz until smooth, then add the ice cubes and blitz again until smooth, to finish. Serve straight away.

TIP
Feel free to swap the whole milk for any other type of milk: almond milk, semi-skimmed, non-dairy… It may change the consistency of the smoothie, but it will taste just as good.

turn over to see the smoothies (from left to right): The "Glow Up" Smoothie; Apple × Blackberry Crumble Smoothie; Biggy Brekky Smoothie; Smooooooooth Talker; and Vibey

Don't Let Me Go Green

Serves 4
Skill Level: light work
You will need a juicer

1 large cucumber
2 large celery sticks
2.5cm piece fresh root
    ginger, peeled
6 large Granny Smith apples
4 large pears
juice of 1–2 lemons, to taste

My mum is an avid juicer. If it was up to her, she'd juice everything. One time she made a broccoli juice and let's just say that that one was in the fridge for a while. Nah, but in all honesty her juice-making is world class, so here are a few recipes she has come up with that we would love to share with you lot.

JUICE THOSE GREENS
Put all the ingredients through your juicer except the lemon juice. Pour the juice into a large bowl or measuring jug and add the lemon juice, starting with the juice of one lemon and tasting it as you go. Store in the fridge until ready to drink (it will keep for up to 2 days).

TIP
The lemon juice helps the juice stay fresh for as long as possible. Mum would suggest drinking it within the next couple of days. I was writing this recipe right next to her on the sofa and she also said:

"The quantities of the ingredients are interchangeable, so if you want it to be less sweet, reduce the amount of fruit and up the veg. And if you want it sweeter, you know what to do. ADD SALTED CARAMEL! Joking, joking…"

Refresher Fresher

Serves 4
Skill Level: light work
You will need a juicer

12 Granny Smith apples
a large handful of basil leaves
juice of 3 limes
3 tbsp agave syrup

I honestly didn't know how nice basil was in juices until recently. Basil almost has its own sweetness, but it still holds onto its savoury notes alongside the green apple, agave syrup and the sharpness of lime here. Trust me, this is a winner. It's super light and refreshing and you can drink it by the gallon (but then that means going through a shed-load of apples and sooooooo much basil… a glass would be better).

QUICK ONE
Pass the apples and basil through your juicer. Pour the juice into a large bowl or measuring jug and stir in the lime juice and syrup. Store in the fridge until ready to drink. It will keep for up to 2–3 days.

"I'm an expert juicer, you know. If you want it to be slightly thinner, and to be shared with more people, add a couple splashes of almond milk."

Classically Orange

Serves 4
Skill Level: light work
You will need a juicer

10–12 large carrots
4 large Gala apples
6 large oranges, peeled
5cm piece fresh root
    ginger, peeled
5cm piece fresh turmeric
juice of 1–2 lemons, to taste

Correct me if I'm wrong, but when you start to like juices with carrots in, irrelevant of your age, you have reached adulthood!

JUICE THAT ORANGE

Put all the ingredients through your juicer except the lemon juice. Pour the juice into a large bowl or measuring jug and add the lemon juice, starting with the juice of one lemon and tasting it as you go. Store in fridge until ready to drink. It will keep for up to 2 days.

The Heart-Shaped Herb Juice

Serves 4
Skill Level: light work
You will need a juicer

6 raw beetroots, peeled
5cm piece fresh root ginger, peeled
4 crisp apples (such as Pink Lady)
300g purple grapes
a small bunch of basil leaves
2 limes, peeled (skin
    and pith removed)
cracked black pepper, to taste

Okay, this drink won't give you super strength or speed but it's purple and tasty. Beetroot stains, trust me I know: 'Av a look at your tongue after you drink this juice. We ain't talking Slush Puppies, we're talking about a perfect midday drink to keep you going!

LET'S GOOO

Pass everything through your juicer, except the black pepper. Pour the juice into a large bowl or measuring jug, give the juice a couple of twists of black pepper, stir again, and store in the fridge until ready to drink. It will keep for up to 2–3 days.

Quick Fix

Veggie Medley

Serves 4
Skill Level: light work
You will need a juicer

2 broccoli stalks
1 large cucumber
2 celery sticks
8 small carrots
1 large red pepper, seeded
juice of 1 lemon

I don't know how madre and I managed to compromise on a recipe consisting of broccoli. I admit I've been taking the mickey out of this ingredient being in a juice, but the honest truth is that if it's blended with other cool ingredients, it's healthy and well tasty, too. Go on then – get your five-a-day in.

EAT YOUR GREENS

Pass everything through your juicer, apart from the lemon juice. Pour the juice into a large bowl or measuring jug and stir in the lemon juice. Store in the fridge until ready to drink. It will keep for up to 2–3 days.

**turn over to see the juices (glasses from left to right):
Don't Let Me Go Green; The Heart-Shaped Herb Juice;
Veggie Medley; Classically Orange; and Refresher Fresher**

Quick Fix

Chilli Cheese Toastie

2 large eggs
3 tbsp whole milk
½ tsp smoked paprika
4 slices brioche
4 tbsp chilli jam
4 slices Gouda
1 tbsp unsalted butter
1 tbsp vegetable oil
fine sea salt, to taste
cracked black pepper, to taste
T Soup (page 105) or tinned
    tomato soup, to serve (optional)

You can probably tell by now that I'm a massive fan of comfort food. So, when there is any chance of making comfort food more comforting, hit me up. The first time I had this flavour combination I was in Scotland, and I will never forget it: it was so simple but it hit all the marks: sweet, salty, a little spicy. When you can't really be bothered to cook a proper meal this is perfect for a stay-at-home snack.

Put the eggs, milk and smoked paprika in a bowl and whisk together, season with salt and pepper and pour into a baking dish.

Spread two slices of the brioche each with 2 tablespoons of chilli jam, then top with the Gouda slices. Top with the remaining two slices of brioche.

Dip the sandwiches in the eggy mixture, making sure both sides of the sandwiches are well coated.

Heat the butter and oil in a large frying pan over a medium heat. Add both sandwiches to the pan and cook for 4 minutes on each side, or until golden brown. Remove from the heat.

"Ahhh mate, I tell you what, heat up a tin of tomato soup or make my T Soup, dip the toastie into it, get munching, and thank me later!"

Quick Fix

Ice Cream Brekky Jar

Clustery Granola Pieces
90g unsalted mixed nuts
225g rolled oats
25g sesame seeds
25g sunflower seeds
60ml sunflower oil
50ml runny honey
80g mixed dried berries

Sleeping Porridge
200g rolled oats
1 tsp ground cinnamon
400ml unsweetened almond milk,
    plus extra to serve
100g raisins
1 tsp fine sea salt

Banana Ice Cream
4 large bananas, cut into chunks
1–2 tbsp almond milk

To Finish
200g mixed berries
200g natural yoghurt
honey

Ice cream for breakfast… well, normally it shouldn't be done. My mum wouldn't allow it, but when I told her it was ice cream made of frozen bananas, clustery pieces of goodness and overnight oats, yup, it got the seal of approval! Start making this the night before you want to to eat it – make it in your PJs, I dare ya. And make a larger batch of granola if you like, to keep and use for other brekky dishes.

THE NIGHT BEFORE

CLUSTERY GRANOLA PIECES
Preheat oven to 190°C/Fan 170°C/Gas 5 and line a baking tray with baking paper.

Mix the nuts, oats and seeds in large bowl, then add the oil and honey. Stir with a fork.

Tip the granola onto the lined baking tray and spread it out in a thin layer. Bake for 20 minutes, stirring twice to make sure it bakes evenly, until golden brown. Tip into a bowl and leave to cool, then chuck in those dried berries and pop into an airtight container ready to use tomorrow.

SLEEPY PORRIDGE
Put the oats in a bowl, stir in the cinnamon, almond milk, raisins and salt, cover and put in the fridge until the next day.

Put the banana chunks on a baking tray and pop the tray in the freezer.

THE NEXT DAY

BANANA ICE CREAM
Throw the frozen banana into the bowl of the food-processor and blitz until smooth, adding enough almond milk to give it a creamy consistency.

Loosen the porridge a little with a little almond milk, then divide it between 4 large jars or bowls. Top with mixed berries, a spoonful of the yoghurt, a scoop or two of the banana ice cream and clustery granola pieces. Add a drizzle of honey and enjoy your breakfast!

"See? I told you ice cream can be healthy!"

T Soup

30g unsalted butter
2 medium onions, chopped
3 garlic cloves, crushed
2 carrots, finely diced
2 celery sticks, finely chopped
7 soft sun-dried tomatoes,
　　roughly chopped
4 x 400g tins plum tomatoes
750ml vegetable stock
1 tbsp caster sugar, or to taste
210g soured cream
fine sea salt, to taste
cracked black pepper, to taste
Chilli Cheese Toasties (page 101),
　　to serve (optional)

Tomato soup is hands-down one of my favourite soups… ever. It's rich, comforting and such a massive crowd-pleaser. Even your neighbour's sister's dog, cat, cousin, or pet pigeon will love it. Especially with my Chilli Cheese Toastie (see page 101). YUM!

Melt the butter in a large saucepan over a low heat, add the onions, garlic, carrots and celery and cook for about 10 minutes until softened. Add the sun-dried tomatoes and tinned tomatoes, vegetable stock, sugar and some salt and pepper, bring to the boil, then reduce the heat and simmer for 10 minutes, until the tomatoes have broken down.

Remove from the heat and use a stick blender to blitz the soup, or whizz it in a food-processor, then add half the soured cream, stir it in and place back over the heat for 2 minutes, to heat through.

Serve the soup in warm bowls, topped with the rest of the soured cream and a Chilli Cheese Toastie (if you like).

"Nice one."

Quick Fix

Proper Brekky Muffin

4 slices American-style cheese
4 large eggs
4 English muffins, cut in half
fine sea salt, to taste
cracked black pepper, to taste

Breakfast Patties
500g pork or beef mince
2 tbsp dried mixed herbs
1 tsp cracked black pepper
1 tsp fine sea salt
1 tsp garlic granules
1 tbsp soft light brown sugar
pinch of ground cloves
4 tbsp vegetable oil

Beany Hash
400g potatoes (skin on)
1 x 415g tin baked beans
dried mixed herbs, to taste
60g salted butter, melted
5 tbsp sunflower oil

Okay, I have a confession to make. I may have had one of these on Christmas day. This recipe brings back a shed-load of memories: for a Friday treat when I was young, just before I went to school, I would have a sausage and egg muffin with the crunchiest of hash browns (maybe with a little BBQ sauce, too). Fast forward a few years and I've made my own version – one to remember!

BREAKFAST PATTIES

Mix all the patty ingredients (except the oil) together in a large bowl, using your hands to make sure all the ingredients are well incorporated.

Divide the mix evenly into four and shape into flattened patties, making them slightly larger than your muffins because they will shrink while cooking.

Heat the oil in a large skillet or frying pan over a medium-high heat. Cook the patties in batches, frying them for 3 minutes on one side, or until well browned, then flipping them over and frying for a further 3 minutes until browned on both sides and cooked through. Remove from the heat.

Now here's the good part. Once you've flipped each patty, top each one with a slice of cheese (while it's still in the pan) and the residual heat should melt the cheese. Transfer to a plate and keep warm.

BEANY HASH

Cook the whole potatoes in a large saucepan of boiling salted water for about 10 minutes, then drain and set aside to cool. Drain the baked beans in a sieve, catching the sauce from the tin in a bowl underneath. Set aside the drained baked bean sauce.

Coarsely grate the potatoes into a separate bowl, discarding any potato skin left in your hand once you've grated the potato. Season well with salt, pepper and mixed herbs. Add the drained baked beans and just over half of the melted butter.

turn over

Mix well and divide the mixture into eight patties, roughly the same width as the cooked patties. You only need four patties for this recipe, so keep the remaining patties in the fridge or freezer – it's a great thing to have in your freezer to pull out when you have people round. Heat the oil and the rest of the melted butter in a frying pan over a medium heat. Once the butter and oil are sizzling, add the beany hash patties and fry gently for 2 minutes 30 seconds on each side until crisp and golden. Transfer to a plate.

EGGS

To get that authentic breakfast-egg shape, heat the same pan over a medium heat with 1 tablespoon of vegetable oil, grease or spray the egg rings with oil and place them in the skillet or pan (if you only have one egg ring, fry the eggs one at a time).

Crack the eggs into the rings, add a couple of tablespoons of water to the pan and cover with a lid. Cook for 2 minutes, or until your egg is cooked to your liking: cook for 1 minute for a runny egg, a little bit longer for a slightly runny egg, then longer than that… yup, that egg is not running. I like my eggs to be walking – in other words, well-cooked with a runny yolk, and not overdone. Transfer to a plate and set aside.

ASSEMBLE

Place the muffins on a baking tray cut side up and grill, or stick them in the toaster.

Top four of the muffin halves with meat patties, then egg, then a beany hash patty. Top with a muffin lid.

"Wait, wait, wait. Take that muffin lid off, get that baked bean sauce, warm it through and give each muffin hash a cheeky drizzle. Wrap each muffin in a bit of baking paper, grab your orange juice, and off you go!"

TIP

If you can't get hold of egg rings, just fry your eggs without the rings. They will be just as tasty.

MFP (Mince Fry Pies)

600g plain flour, plus
    extra for dusting
1 tsp fine sea salt
1 tsp ground mixed spice
grated zest of 1 large orange
375g unsalted butter, frozen
    (put it in the freezer the
    night before you need it)
190–200ml cold water
sunflower oil, for deep-frying
600g homemade or
    shop-bought mincemeat
1 large egg, beaten

Brandy Glaze
250g icing sugar, sifted
75ml whole milk
75ml double cream
1 tbsp brandy

There is a certain takeaway restaurant that sells legendary apple pies. The reason they are legendary? They are fried, so have super crisp pastry and a piping hot filling, but hey, I've switched it up a little bit with this super simple but tasty Christmassy filling. The brandy glaze is optional, of course, but I can promise you it takes these pies to the next level. Enjoy!

PASTRY

Put the flour in a large bowl and stir in the salt, mixed spice and orange zest.

Grate half the frozen butter into the bowl and give it a quick toss with a table knife or palette knife. Grate in the rest of the butter and mix it through the flour with the knife, too – you want to make sure all the butter is well coated into the flour.

Slowly pour the 190ml cold water into the butter and flour mixture, stirring constantly with the table knife until it comes together and forms a light dough (use the remaining 10ml only if necessary). Bring it together into a ball, handling it as little as possible, then cut it into half and form each half into a rough square. Wrap each piece in clingfilm and place in the fridge to chill for 30 minutes.

Pour sunflower oil into a deep-fat fryer up to the safety markers and heat to 180°C. If you don't have a deep-fat fryer, two-thirds fill a large saucepan and use a cooking thermometer. Line a large plate or baking tray with kitchen paper.

ROLL × FILL

Roll one of the pieces of chilled pastry out into a large rectangular shape on a lightly floured surface until it's about 30 x 24cm and just slightly thicker than a £1 coin. Cut into 6 equal rectangular slices about 12 x 10cm.

Spoon a couple of heaped tablespoons of mincemeat onto one half of each pastry rectangle. Brush the edges of each rectangle lightly with beaten egg. Fold the pastry over the filling to make a closed pie shape and press the edges together. Seal the edges with the prongs of a fork.

Repeat the same process with the other half of the pastry.

turn over

Quick Fix

FRY 'EM

Deep-fry the pies, two or three at a time, for 2–3 minutes on each side, turning them with tongs, until the pastry is golden brown. Carefully remove the pies with a slotted spoon then transfer to the paper-lined tray or plate to absorb excess oil.

GLAZE

Place all the fried pies on a wire rack with a baking tray underneath it, while they are still warm. Combine all the ingredients for the glaze in a bowl until well combined.

Use a pastry brush to coat one side of each pie with the glaze, allow it to dry for 5–10 minutes, then flip them over and brush the other side with glaze.

"If you fancy a little extra sweetness, go for two coatings of glaze."

If you have time, pop the pies on a baking tray in a 180°C/Fan 160°C/Gas 4 oven for a couple of minutes. The glaze should harden and become shiny. Cool, right?

Quick Fix

Stackin' Sundays

The Stack
250g wholemeal or rye flour
60g porridge oats
4 tsp baking powder
1 tsp fine sea salt
2 tsp ground cinnamon
¼ tsp freshly grated nutmeg
4 large egg whites
480–500ml unsweetened
    almond milk
120g Greek yoghurt
80g light muscovado sugar
2 tsp vanilla extract
    or vanilla bean paste
unsalted butter, vegetable
    or sunflower oil, or cooking
    spray, for frying

Blueberry Filler
150g fresh blueberries
3 tbsp water
runny honey, to taste, plus
    extra to serve

Caramelised Banana Topper
50g unsalted butter
4 large bananas, cut into
    1cm chunks
caster sugar, for sprinkling

To Serve
peanut butter of choice
Greek yoghurt (or
    yoghurt of choice)
200g toasted pecans,
    roughly chopped

When my mum and I are both in on a Sunday, I'm on breakfast duty. I have been making this dish for years, and it's always been typed up on my phone, but now it's time to give it proper double-page spread glory. It's healthy-ish, wholesome and tasty. You just can't go wrong. Oh yeah, I forgot to tell you, this recipe inspired one of my challenges for… you know what I'm talking about! Enjoy.

Preheat oven to 150°C/Fan 130°C/Gas 2.

MAKE THE BATTER
Tip the flour, oats, baking powder, salt and spices into a bowl and give the mixture a quick mix. Set to one side.

Put the egg whites and milk in another bowl and whisk until just combined. Give the yoghurt and sugar a quick mix together until there are no lumps, add them to the egg and milk mixture, then add the vanilla. Mix just until well combined. Add the dry ingredients to the wet ingredients and fold together until well combined. For the sake of the pancakes, please don't over-mix the batter: it'll make them dense.

FRY THE PANCAKES
Heat a frying pan over a medium heat and coat the surface of the pan with a little butter, oil or cooking spray. Once the pan is hot, pour about 60ml of batter into the pan. Cook for about 1 minute, until the pancake starts to look set around the edges and bubbles start to form on the top. Flip it over and cook for a further 2 minutes.

Repeat the process with the rest of the batter, re-greasing the pan each time: the mixture should make 12 pancakes. Pop all the pancakes on a baking tray, spread out, and place in the low oven to keep them warm.

BANANA TOPPER
Melt the butter in a frying pan over a medium heat. Toss in your banana chunks and fry for 1–2 minutes until lightly browned, then sprinkle with a little sugar and fry for a few more minutes until caramelised.

Keep the bananas warm on a baking paper-lined baking tray in the low oven, along with the pancakes.

turn over

BLUEBERRY FILLING

Tip your blueberries into a saucepan with the water and a drizzle of honey (to taste). Cook gently over a low heat for 3–5 minutes until warmed through.

STACKIN' SUNDAY TIME

Okay, believe it or not there is an art to stacking pancakes. You have to make sure that with every mouthful you take, you have a taste of everything, so here goes:

Place one pancake on a serving plate and spread it generously with peanut butter, then drizzle with honey. Spread the honey into the peanut butter and top with some blueberries. Top with a second pancake, repeating the peanut butter, honey and blueberries, then do this again with a third, but instead of finishing it off with another pancake, plop a generous dollop of yoghurt onto the peanut butter, honey and blueberries. Repeat with three more servings. Then, yes you guessed it, top with those caramelised bananas. For an extra earthy, toasty, crunchy texture finish off with a scattering of some toasted pecans.

"Stackin' Sunday over and out!"

Quick Fix

The Hot Chocolate Trio

The White
1 litre whole milk
200g white chocolate,
    broken into pieces
2 tsp vanilla extract
    or vanilla bean paste
8 tbsp Biscoff spread

The Milk
600ml whole milk
100g milk chocolate,
    broken into pieces
8 tbsp hazelnut spread
4 tbsp hazelnut liqueur (optional)

The Dark
550ml whole milk
180ml double cream
200g dark chocolate,
    broken into pieces
100ml Irish cream

To Serve
whipped cream
biscuits of choice
extra dark chocolate, for shaving

I don't often drink hot chocolate, but when I do, I go to town the cheeky way. Instead of just going for typical cocoa powder with milk, I use actual chocolate and lots of different flavours. Here, you've got all three – white, milk, dark. Let's go.

To make each hot chocolate, just put all the ingredients in a saucepan over a medium-low heat and bring to a gentle boil, whisking constantly until smooth, then pour into cups, top with whipped cream, a couple of crushed biscuits or chocolate shavings – you pick.

"The award for the shortest but tastiest recipe, out of any recipe Liam has made, goes tooooooooooooooooooooooo..."

Quick Fix

Puddings

04

The 3-M (Miso × Maple × Macadamia) Scoop

Ice cream
330ml whole milk
500ml double cream
2 vanilla pods, split lengthways
5 large egg yolks
2 tbsp caster sugar
150ml maple syrup
50g white miso paste

Macadamia Praline
200g caster sugar
4 tbsp water
80g unsalted macadamia nuts

One thing I love about ice cream is that the flavour combinations are endless. Sweet, savoury and even salty ice creams can be served for pud – you name it. For this recipe the main ingredients are miso paste, maple syrup and macadamia. Get your page tags at the ready – this one is a keeper. Make the custard for the ice cream at least a day before you want to serve the ice cream.

DAY 1

CUSTARD

Pour the milk and cream into a large saucepan. Scrape the seeds from the vanilla pods and add the seeds and the pods to the pan. Warm over a low heat until just below boiling point.

While the milk and cream mixture is warming up, put your egg yolks and caster sugar into a large, heatproof bowl and mix until well combined.

Just as the milk and cream mixture reaches a simmer, remove it from the heat and slowly pour it into the bowl of egg yolks in a slow and steady stream, whisking constantly.

Pour the custard back into the saucepan and cook it over a low heat for 10–15 minutes, stirring constantly with a large wooden spoon, until it thickens.

"There's a really good scrambled egg recipe in the book but this isn't it, so keep stirring."

Once it thickly coats the back of the spoon, your custard is ready. Strain the custard through a fine sieve into a heatproof bowl to remove the vanilla pods. Add the maple syrup and miso paste and mix until thoroughly combined. Place a sheet of clingfilm directly on the surface of the custard, to prevent any skin from forming, then allow the custard to cool completely. Pop in the fridge overnight to chill.

turn over

DAY II

MACADAMIA PRALINE
Put the caster sugar in a heavy-based frying pan with the water and heat gently over a medium-low heat until the sugar dissolves and the liquid becomes clear, swirling the pan if necessary to distribute the sugar evenly. Crank up the heat and let the mixture bubble for about 10 minutes (don't stir) until it is a deep golden caramel colour. Once you smell caramel, you know it's ready.

Drop the nuts into the pan and swirl them around to evenly coat them with the caramel, then pour onto a sheet of baking paper and leave to cool.

CHURN BABY CHURN
Churn the custard in an ice-cream machine according to the manufacturer's instructions. Once the praline has firmed up, break the praline into pieces and smash it with a rolling pin.

Once your ice cream is churned, pop it in a freezer-proof container. Tip just over half of the praline into the ice cream and swirl with a spoon until it is well incorporated. Put the container back in the freezer, covered with a lid, to freeze until solid.

ASSEMBLE
About 10 minutes before serving, remove the ice cream from the freezer so it softens slightly. When ready to serve, top each scoop with a little bit of praline or, if it's a free-for-all, sprinkle the leftover praline on top of the whole lot.

"Scoops × spoons at the ready!"

Rhubarb × Custard Cheesecake

Biscuit Base
260g ginger biscuits,
    smashed into crumbs
90g unsalted butter, melted,
    plus extra for greasing
4 tbsp finely diced stem ginger

Rhubarb Compote
250g rhubarb, trimmed and
    cut into 5cm chunks
grated zest of 1 large orange
75g caster sugar
4 tbsp water

Cheesecake Filling
900g full-fat cream cheese
200g golden caster sugar
200g soured cream
1 tbsp plain flour
3 tbsp custard powder
1 tsp vanilla extract
    or vanilla bean paste
3 large eggs
yellow food colouring
pink food colouring
400ml whipping cream,
    to serve

Yup, this flavour combination has to make another appearance.
A cheesecake version of the old-time favourite pairing of rhubarb
and custard, with the added twist of a stem gingery base.

Preheat oven to 200°C/Fan 180°C/Gas 6. Grease the base and
sides of the springform tin then line with baking paper.

GINGERY GINGER BASE
Put the biscuit crumbs in a bowl with the melted butter and diced
stem ginger. Mix until combined. Transfer to the lined tin and
press the coated crumbs firmly into the base. Bake for 8 minutes,
until firm. Remove from the oven and set aside.

RHUBARB
Put the rhubarb in a large saucepan with the orange zest, caster
sugar and water. Place the saucepan over a medium heat and
bring to the boil, then reduce the heat to low and simmer for
5–10 minutes, or until the rhubarb is soft. Blitz the cooked
rhubarb in a food-processor or blender until smooth. Transfer
to a heatproof bowl and set aside to cool.

CHEESECAKE FILLING
Beat the cream cheese in the bowl of a stand mixer to loosen
it a little. (You can do this with a hand-held electric whisk or
spoon if you prefer.) Add the sugar and soured cream and mix
to combine. Combine the flour, custard powder and vanilla, then
add to the cream cheese mixture before adding the eggs one at
a time, mixing gently between each addition until the eggs are
incorporated into the mixture.

Divide the cheesecake mixture evenly between two bowls. Colour
one bowl with yellow food colouring, starting with just a couple of
drops then adding more to increase the colour intensity, then the
other with pink. Don't go crazy on the colouring though – just add
enough so it still looks super tasty and not too bright.

turn over

Puddings

Fold half of the rhubarb compote into the pink cheesecake filling (set aside the remaining compote to serve). Using two dessertspoons, fill your cheesecake tin with the two cheesecake mixtures, spoonful by spoonful, alternating between the two mixtures (in layers or dollops, as you wish). Using a metal skewer or a table knife, swirl the mixtures together in a figure-of-eight motion at the top.

"It looks so great when it comes out of the oven, I tell you."

BAKE

Place the cheesecake in the middle of the oven and bake for 10 minutes. Reduce the oven temperature to 130°C/110°C fan/ Gas ½ and bake for a further 1¼ hours, until cooked (it should have a little cheeky wobble in the middle).

Switch off the oven and leave the cheesecake inside, with the door closed, for 1 hour. Then, open the oven door and leave the cheesecake inside with the door slightly ajar for another hour.

Remove the cheesecake from the oven, cover with a clean tea towel and leave to cool at room temperature for another hour (the long cooling process will help prevent your cheesecake from cracking).

Once the cheesecake is completely cool, carefully remove it from the tin and peel off the baking paper. Place it on a large serving plate. Whip the whipping cream to soft peaks and swirl in the remaining rhubarb compote. Spoon onto the cheesecake and serve in slices.

TIP

To help prevent your cheesecake cracking, place a roasting tray at the bottom of the oven, filled halfway with boiling water from the kettle, before putting the cheesecake in the oven. This keeps the cheesecake cooking at a certain temperature and nothing over. Though if it does crack, it's not the end of the world – it tastes the same!

Lasagne for Dessert. Wait, what?

Lasagne Cream and Sheets
500g ricotta
125ml double cream
90g caster sugar
1 tsp almond extract
3 large eggs, lightly beaten
20g unsalted butter
6 dried lasagne sheets

Fruit Ragu
1 Bramley apple, peeled, cored and diced
2 Granny Smith apples, peeled, cored and diced
2 Pink Lady apples, peeled, cored and diced
200g fresh blackberries
grated zest and juice of 1 unwaxed lemon
50g unsalted butter
100g caster sugar
2 tsp ground cinnamon
1 tsp vanilla extract or vanilla bean paste
¼ tsp fine sea salt

Almond Crumble
160g plain flour
160g soft light brown sugar
50g flaked almonds, plus extra, toasted, to serve
½ tsp ground cinnamon
80g unsalted butter, cold, diced

White Chocolate "Béchamel Sauce" Custard
300ml double cream
600ml whole milk
4 large egg yolks
3 tbsp cornflour
150g caster sugar
1 tsp vanilla extract or vanilla bean paste
100g white chocolate, broken into pieces
½ tsp ground cinnamon
25g unsalted butter, cold, diced

Playing with food is one of my strengths as a baker, so why don't we turn something that's traditionally a main course into a dessert? My uncle's pal, Chris, came up with this amazing idea for a sweet lasagne for a work baking competition. As soon as I found out about it, I just had to make my own. Chris Doyle, you're a genius.

Preheat oven to 180°C/Fan 160°C/Gas 4.

LASAGNE CREAM
Put the ricotta, double cream, caster sugar and almond extract in a medium bowl and mix together until smooth. Add the eggs, a little at time, beating between each addition, then pop in the fridge until ready to use.

FRUIT RAGU
Put the diced apples in a large saucepan with the blackberries. Add the lemon zest and juice to the saucepan along with the rest of the ingredients. Place over a medium-low heat and cook, stirring occasionally, for 20–25 minutes until the fruit is cooked through but still has a bite to it. Transfer to a clean bowl and leave to cool.

DESSERT LASAGNE SHEETS
Bring a large saucepan of salted water to the boil and add the butter. Add the lasagne sheets to the water, one at a time, and stir gently. Boil for 5 minutes or until the pasta is tender. Drain.

Spread a third of the fruit ragu over the bottom of the baking dish.

Lay 3 lasagne sheets on top of the ragu, then spread half of the ricotta mixture over the sheets. Top with the remaining 3 lasagne sheets and spread with another third of the fruit ragu and the rest of the ricotta mixture. Finish with the fruit ragu on top.

ALMOND CRUMBLE
Stir together the flour, soft brown sugar, flaked almonds and cinnamon in a bowl. Add the butter and mix it in with your fingertips until the mixture is crumbly. Sprinkle the crumble mixture over the fruit ragu.

Bake for 45 minutes, until the ragu is bubbling and the crumble is golden brown. Remove from the oven and leave to cool for 15 minutes.

turn over

Puddings

WHITE CHOCOLATE "BÉCHAMEL SAUCE" CUSTARD

Pour the cream and milk into a large saucepan and warm over a low heat until just below boiling point.

Meanwhile, whisk the egg yolks in a large heatproof bowl with the cornflour, sugar and vanilla until well combined. Slowly pour the hot milk and cream into the sugar mixture, whisking constantly.

Pour the custard back into the pan and cook over a low heat, stirring, until the custard has thickened – it should be thick enough to coat the back of a wooden spoon. Finally, remove the pan from the heat and pass the custard through a sieve into a heatproof bowl. Chuck in your white chocolate, cinnamon and butter and stir: the residual heat should melt the chocolate and butter.

Cut a square of the dessert lasagne, drizzle over some white chocolate custard and serve with extra toasted almonds.

Mum's Dessert Pots

Baked Fruit
4 Granny Smith apples, peeled, cored and quartered
12 plums, halved and stoned
2 tsp ground cinnamon
juice of 1 lemon
juice of 2 oranges, plus 2 pared strips of orange zest
200ml brandy
5 allspice berries
65g soft light brown sugar
50g unsalted butter

Crumble
150g plain flour
125g unsalted butter, cold, diced
35g demerara sugar

Chocolate Shells
500g dark chocolate (70% cocoa solids), chopped
3 tbsp runny honey
200g crème fraîche
30g unsalted shelled pistachios, roughly chopped, to serve

My cake heart skipped a beat when Mum told me one year that she didn't want a cake for her birthday… I know! Insane! She wanted something more dessert-ish, so I went to the drawing board, sketched up some ideas and here's the result… nice one!

FRUITY CRUMBLY MIDDLE
Preheat oven to 200°C/Fan 180°C/Gas 6.

First, prepare the baked fruit. Put the apples and plums in a roasting tin with the cinnamon, lemon juice, pared orange peel and brandy. Pour the orange juice over the fruit and tuck the pieces of orange peel underneath the fruit. Tuck the allspice berries under the fruit, too.

Sprinkle over the sugar and add knobs of the butter on top. Bake for 10 minutes while you make the crumble mixture.

Put the flour, butter and sugar in the bowl of a food-processor and pulse until the mixture resembles coarse breadcrumbs (alternatively make the crumble mixture by hand, using your fingertips to rub the butter into the flour before stirring in the sugar). Sprinkle the mixture into a baking tray and spread it out.

When the fruit has been cooking for 10 minutes, reduce the oven temperature to 180°C/Fan 160°C/Gas 4. Put the tray of crumble mixture in the oven and cook everything for a further 10–15 minutes, until the fruit has taken on some colour, the juices have started to reduce to a syrup, and the crumble is golden brown and moves when you shake the tray from side to side. Transfer the fruit to a heatproof dish using a slotted spoon, discard the orange peel strips and allspice berries and set aside to cool. Reserve the syrup.

CHOCOLATE SHELLS
To make the chocolate shells, melt 330g of the chocolate in a heatproof bowl over a pan of barely simmering water (making sure the bottom of the bowl isn't touching the water), until it reaches 45–50°C on the food thermometer. Then, add the remaining chopped chocolate and remove the bowl from the pan. Stir the chocolate off the heat until it is completely melted and the temperature reads 31–32°C.

Pour the chocolate into 6 of the dome mould holes, give it a swirl around to coat the sides and pour the excess chocolate back into the bowl. Place the moulds in the fridge for about 15 minutes, to allow the chocolate to set.

Puddings

Once the chocolate is firm, bring the remaining melted chocolate back to 31–32°C over the pan of simmering water then use it to apply a second coating to each of the four moulds. Allow to set for 10 minutes in the fridge, then carefully remove the chocolate shells from the mould.

ASSEMBLE

Divide the cooled fruit equally between the chocolate shells and sprinkle a generous amount of crumble over the fruit.

Stir the honey and crème fraîche together in a bowl.

To serve (chilled or at room temperature – don't fill the chocolate shells until ready to serve), place a filled chocolate shell on each serving plate and drizzle over a little of the reserved fruit syrup. Finally, top with a dollop of the honey and crème fraîche and sprinkle over a little chopped pistachio. We like tucking into the crumble first, then eating the bowl at the end.

"There's always spare crumble and fruit filling going, so when you're ready to impress, make a few more chocolate shells and you've got a super simple and tasty dessert. If you're pushed for time, don't worry about the chocolate shells: the deconstructed crumble has enough flavour to hold its own... see what I did there? Word play!"

The Pinwheel

Spiced Crème Pat
350ml whole milk
½ tsp vanilla extract
　　or vanilla bean paste
¼ tsp freshly grated nutmeg
¼ tsp ground cloves
¼ tsp ground turmeric
¼ tsp ground ginger
75g soft dark brown sugar
3 large egg yolks
30g cornflour
30g unsalted butter, diced

Apple Filling
200g stoned Medjool
　　dates, chopped
300ml orange juice
1 large Bramley apple
1 Granny Smith apple
1 Pink Lady apple
juice of 1 lemon
20g unsalted butter
30g golden caster sugar
1 tsp ground cinnamon
1 tbsp cornflour
2 tbsp water

Pastry
2 x 270g packs filo pastry (12 sheets)
125g unsalted butter, melted
1 large egg, beaten
golden caster sugar, for sprinkling

Orange Caramel
40ml water
115g caster sugar
40g unsalted butter
65ml double cream
¼ tsp vanilla extract
　　or vanilla bean paste
½ tsp fine sea salt
grated zest of 1 orange

Candied Cashews
50g caster sugar
15g unsalted butter
125g whole cashews

To Serve
double cream or ice cream

Inspired by the Moroccan m'hanncha ("snake pie"), this is rocking with caramel, apples and spiced custard, all wrapped up in one of my favourites – filo pastry. Don't get me wrong, I love making pastry from scratch, but sometimes it's better to spend more time enjoying the final bake with your pals and family. Let's get on it! Make the crème pat the day before if you can, so it has time to properly chill.

SPICED CRÈME PAT
Pour the milk into a large saucepan and add the vanilla, nutmeg and other spices. Warm over a low heat until just below boiling point.

Meanwhile, whisk the sugar, egg yolks and cornflour together in a large heatproof bowl.

Slowly pour the warm milk into the egg yolk mixture, whisking constantly.

Pour the custard back into the pan and cook over a low heat, stirring constantly with a wooden spoon, for 10–15 minutes until the mixture thickens. When it's ready it should be thick enough to coat the back of the spoon.

Remove from the heat and pass the custard through a sieve into a heatproof bowl. Add the butter and stir until melted, then place a sheet of clingfilm on the surface of the custard to prevent a skin from forming. Set aside until cool, then place the custard in the fridge to chill (overnight if possible).

APPLE × DATES = MATES
Pop the dates and the orange juice in a bowl and leave to soak until ready to use.

Peel, cut and dice all the apples and place in a large saucepan. Add the lemon juice to the pan, toss, then add the butter, sugar and cinnamon.

Put the cornflour and water in a separate bowl and mix with a fork until smooth, then pour it over the apples. Stir and place over a medium-low heat. Cook the apples, stirring occasionally, for about 20 minutes. You want some of the apple chunks to be completely cooked through, but some to keep their bite to them. Taste it and check for sweetness and acidity, adding more sugar or lemon juice if you feel it needs it.

Put the apple filling in a heatproof bowl and allow to cool. Strain the dates then stir them into the apple filling.

Line a baking tray with baking paper.

"Alright, let's get this cracking. You need a little space for this."

ASSEMBLE THE PINWHEEL
Unwrap the filo and cover the sheets with a clean, damp tea towel so they don't dry out. Put the melted butter and beaten egg in separate bowls close by, at the ready, with two pastry brushes.

Quickly lay 4 sheets of the filo pastry end to end, running lengthways along your work surface. Brush a generous amount of melted butter all over the sheets and overlap each sheet by about 10cm. Place 3 more sheets of filo over the 4 sheets you've just brushed with butter then brush them with more butter. (You will have some spare sheets to use in case there are any cracks.)

Take the clingfilm off the custard and give it a good whisk with a hand-held electric whisk until it has a piping consistency. Spoon the custard into the piping bag and pipe a strip of custard down the length of the filo, leaving 5cm free on either side. Spoon scoops of the apple filling down the filo too, next to the custard. Brush the beaten egg along the filo edges and fold the ends over the filling. Starting from one end, roll the filo over the filling, working your way along until you have a filo sausage. Start to coil your filo sausage until it resembles a spiral. This is when cracks may appear: if you see any, patch them up with your leftover filo, brushing it with more melted butter to help them stick.

Carefully slide the pinwheel onto the lined baking tray, cover loosely with clingfilm and chill in the fridge for 1 hour.

CARAMEL ON THE FLY
Put the water in a saucepan, then gradually add the caster sugar, stirring to combine it evenly with the water. Place the pan over a medium heat and heat for about 10 minutes until the sugar has dissolved to a caramel and turned a deep amber colour (don't stir once the pan is over the heat).

turn over

Puddings

Take the pan off the heat, add the butter, then return to the heat and stir until the butter has completely melted and is well combined.

Remove from the heat again, add the double cream, vanilla, salt and orange zest, and mix again. Return to the heat for a few more seconds, then pour into a heatproof bowl and set aside.

CANDIED CASHEWS
Line a baking sheet with baking paper.

Put the caster sugar and butter in a heavy-based saucepan and place over a medium heat. Heat for about 5 minutes, stirring constantly, until the sugar is caramelised.

Time to move quickly: tip the cashews into the syrup, stir to coat, then tip onto the lined baking sheet and separate the nuts with a clean spatula. Set aside to cool, then chop them into smallish pieces. Place in a bowl and you're good to go.

BAKE
Preheat oven to 200°C/Fan 180°C/Gas 6.

Brush the pinwheel with the beaten egg, sprinkle it with golden caster sugar, then pop the tray on the middle shelf of the oven and bake for 30–35 minutes until golden brown and crisp.

Remove from the oven and allow to cool for 20 minutes, as the filling will be very hot.

Top the pinwheel with a squiggle of the orange caramel and the chopped candied cashews.

There is only one thing you can serve this dessert with – double cream. Okay, maybe ice cream.

Hard Dough Bread ×
Butter "Twiss Up" Pudding

Puddings

Spiced Butter
120g unsalted butter, softened,
  plus extra for greasing
1 tsp fine sea salt
½ tsp ground cinnamon
½ tsp ground cloves
¼ tsp ground ginger
¼ tsp freshly grated nutmeg
grated zest of 1 orange

Punchy Custard
440ml can Irish stout
2 large eggs, plus 6 egg yolks
4 tbsp golden caster sugar
300ml whole milk
300ml double cream
1 tsp vanilla extract
  or vanilla bean paste
12 thick slices (about 600g)
  Caribbean hard dough bread
200g guava jam
4 tbsp demerara sugar
custard or single cream,
  to serve (optional)

Rum-glazed Pineapple
100g soft dark brown sugar
2 tbsp dark spiced rum
1 pineapple, peeled, cored and flesh
  cut into 2cm chunks (you should
  have about 300g chunks)

I think bread and butter pudding is underrated. It's a massive crowd-pleaser, wholesome and perfect for adding your own flavour twist to. In this version, I want you to forget normal sliced bread – try Caribbean hard dough bread: it's richer and softer, and more puddingy. With a few extra twists this pud is an absolute game changer. Oh yeah, and just in case, be very close to a sofa, bed or cushiony floor; you might want a cheeky kip after eating this.

SPICE UP YOUR BUTTER
Beat the butter in a bowl until creamy, then add all the remaining ingredients and mix again until everything is well incorporated. Set aside at room temperature until ready to use.

PUNCHY CUSTARD
Pour the Irish stout into a small saucepan and place it over a medium heat. Bring to the boil, then reduce the heat and simmer for 20–25 minutes, until it has reduced to 50–60ml. Remove from the heat and set aside to cool.

Grease the ovenproof dish with butter.

Whisk the eggs, egg yolks and caster sugar together in a bowl.

Pour the milk, cream, vanilla and cooled, reduced Irish stout into a saucepan and place over a medium heat. Cook, stirring, until the mixture just starts to boil, then remove from the heat and pour it over the egg mixture, stirring to combine until smooth. Set aside.

BE GENEROUS NOW
Spread both sides of the sliced bread with the spiced butter, trying not to leave any bits unbuttered, as these could catch and burn in the oven during baking. Then, spread one side of each slice with guava jam. Set aside while you make the rum-glazed pineapple.

RUMMY YUMMY PINEAPPLE
Put the dark brown sugar in a shallow, heavy-based pan over a medium-high heat. Add the rum and swirl the pan occasionally to encourage the sugar to melt. Once melted, add the pineapple and allow it to bubble in the caramel for about 10 minutes, stirring occasionally, until it looks nicely sticky.

turn over

ASSEMBLE × BAKE

Cut each bread slice in half diagonally and place the halved slices in the dish, almost standing up and with a cheeky little overlap.

Pour the custard over the bread slices and leave the bread to soak for at least 30 minutes (up to 1 hour). When nearly ready to cook, preheat oven to 180°C/Fan 160°C/Gas 4.

Scatter the pineapple pieces over the custard-soaked bread and sprinkle over the demerara sugar. Bake the pudding for 35–40 minutes, until the custard has set and the top of the pudding is golden brown. Remove from the oven and leave to rest for 5–10 minutes, then serve with cream or custard, if you wish.

Fab Terrine

Fun Brown-butter Blondie
165g unsalted butter, plus extra
    for greasing
275g soft light brown sugar
2 large eggs
1 tbsp vanilla extract or
    vanilla bean paste
220g plain flour
1 tsp baking powder
¼ tsp fine sea salt
130g multi-coloured cake sprinkles

Raspberry × Rhubarb Jelly
250g rhubarb, cut into small pieces
grated zest and juice of
    ½ unwaxed lemon
2 tbsp water
50g caster sugar
250g fresh raspberries
2½ gelatine leaves

Greek Yoghurt × Honey Panna Cotta
100ml double cream
100ml whole milk
40g runny honey
seeds from 1 vanilla pod
    (keep the pod)
1 chai tea bag
3 gelatine leaves
100g caster sugar
300g Greek yoghurt

Milky Mousse
65g milk chocolate (35% cocoa
    solids), broken into pieces
½ tsp fine sea salt
2 large eggs
20g caster sugar
2 gelatine leaves
65ml double cream
1 tbsp cocoa powder
50ml whole milk

White Chocolate Bark
200g white chocolate,
    broken into pieces
50g multi-coloured cake sprinkles,
    plus an extra handful to serve

Summer is approaching – well, it was when I was writing this book – so it's berry season! Here, raspberry and rhubarb jelly, honey and yoghurt panna cotta and silky milk chocolate mousse stand proudly on a fun brown-butter blondie base. I tell you what, when you cut it, it will look like that ice lolly, init.

BROWN BUTTER × BAKE

Preheat oven to 190°C/Fan 170°C/Gas 5. Grease the loaf tin and line the base and sides with a sheet of clingfilm as smoothly as possible, leaving a slight overhang around the edges, and line the baking tin with baking paper.

To brown your butter for the blondies, put the butter in a heavy-based saucepan and heat over a medium heat for about 10 minutes until the butter has melted and started to foam, and the milk solids have separated from the fat. Continue to cook the butter, stirring occasionally, until the milk solids have turned brown (almost burnt), and the butter has turned a deep amber colour. Remove from the heat and pour into a heatproof bowl to cool.

Mix the sugar into the cooled brown butter, then add the eggs one at a time, mixing after each addition, followed by the vanilla. Combine the flour, baking powder and salt then tip into the buttery mixture and fold it in. Finally, add the sprinkles and mix them in gently. Tip the blondie mixture into the baking tin and spread it out evenly. Bake for 25–30 minutes, until golden brown and a skewer inserted into the middle comes out clean. Remove from the oven and leave in the tin until it's completely cool.

RASPBERRY × RHUBARB JELLY

Put the rhubarb, lemon juice and zest, water and sugar in a saucepan, add the raspberries, place over a low heat and cook for 5–7 minutes until the raspberries release their juice, the rhubarb softens and the liquid becomes syrupy. Blitz in a food-processor, then pass through a sieve into a bowl (to remove the raspberry seeds).

Weigh the fruit purée and if it is under 600g, top it up with water. Put the fruit purée back in the pan.

turn over for more ingredients

Puddings

143

French Cream Kisses
200ml double cream
2 tbsp caster sugar
½ tsp vanilla extract
    or vanilla bean paste

Soak the gelatine leaves in a bowl of cold water for 5 minutes, until soft. Squeeze the excess water from the softened leaves and add them to the warm purée. Stir the mixture until the gelatine has dissolved, then pour into the clingfilm-lined loaf tin and leave in the fridge for 1½ hours to set.

PANNA COTTA

Put the double cream and milk in a medium saucepan with the honey, scraped vanilla pod and seeds, and tea bag. Heat over a medium-low heat, bring to a gentle simmer, then remove from the heat and leave to stand for a couple of minutes.

Put the gelatine leaves in a bowl of cold water and leave them to soak for 5 minutes, until soft.

Return your "honey milk" to the heat, tip in the caster sugar and stir until just dissolved. Remove from the heat.

Squeeze the excess water from the gelatine leaves and mix them into the warm honey mixture until dissolved. Set aside for 10 minutes.

Tip the Greek yoghurt into a large bowl and beat until it has a creamy consistency. Remove the tea bag and vanilla pod from the "honey milk", pour it into the yoghurt and whisk together until well combined. Tip your panna cotta mixture on top of the set raspberry jelly. Return to the fridge for 1½ hours to set.

MILKY MOUSSE

Melt the milk chocolate with the salt in a heatproof bowl placed over a pan of barely simmering water (making sure the bottom of the bowl doesn't touch the water). Separate the eggs and place the whites and yolks into separate, clean bowls. Add the caster sugar to the yolks and beat until smooth and silky. Remove the bowl of melted chocolate from the pan.

Soak the gelatine leaves in a bowl of cold water.

Whisk the egg whites until they form soft peaks. In a third bowl, whisk the double cream until softly whipped. Add the cocoa powder to the egg yolks and mix, then mix in the cream. Fold in the melted chocolate.

turn over

Gently heat the milk in a heatproof bowl in the microwave or a pan until warm. Squeeze excess water from the softened gelatine leaves, add them to the milk and stir to dissolve. Fold into the double cream mixture and, last but not least, tip your whipped egg whites into the bowl and fold them gently into the chocolate mixture with a metal spoon, using a figure-of-eight motion.

Gently pour the mousse mixture on top of the set panna cotta, level it out, then chill in the fridge for 1½ hours, or until it's almost set (it's going to act like a glue for the blondie layer).

FINAL LAYER × DECORATION
Trim a rectangle of blondie large enough to cover the mousse layer in the tin. Gently place onto the almost-set mousse, wrap the whole tin in more clingfilm and leave to chill for 1–1½ hours.

While the terrine is chilling, make your chocolate bark. Melt the chocolate in a heatproof bowl placed over a pan of barely simmering water (making sure the bottom of the bowl doesn't touch the water). Pour the melted chocolate onto a baking tray, leave it to cool a little until almost set, then scatter over the sprinkles. Place in the fridge and leave in the fridge for 15–30 minutes until set. Once set, break the chocolate slab into triangular shards.

To make French cream kisses, whisk the double cream in a bowl with the caster sugar and vanilla until softly whipped, then place the nozzle into the piping bag, followed by the cream, ready to pipe.

Once the terrine is set, unwrap it, turn the tin upside down onto a serving board and gently remove the tin. Peel off the clingfilm.

Pipe a few "kisses" of whipped cream onto the jelly, then add some chocolate shards. To finish, scatter the extra handful of sprinkles on top.

TIP
You can speed up the setting process by chilling each layer in the freezer for 20 minutes first, then finishing it in the fridge for 30 minutes.

"Fabulous."

Dripping-in-Sauce Pineapple Pudding

Puddings

Pineapple
140g caster sugar
75g unsalted butter
1 large pineapple, peeled,
　cored and cut into 2cm chunks
2 tbsp rum

Sponge
225g self-raising flour
120g soft light brown sugar
125ml whole milk
2 large eggs
80g crystallised ginger, thinly sliced
80g unsalted butter, melted and
　cooled, plus extra for greasing
2 tbsp golden syrup

Topping
1 tsp cornflour
100g soft light brown sugar
85g golden syrup
375ml boiling water

To Serve
Ice cream or double cream
　(optional)

This is pretty much a pineapple upside-down cake that decided to be sensible and show its sponge side, with a whole bunch of different flavours to go along with it.

PINEAPPLE
Preheat oven to 180°C/Fan 160°C/Gas 4 and grease the pie dishes with butter.

Put the caster sugar in a frying pan and heat gently over a low heat, swirling it occasionally by tilting the pan, until the sugar has dissolved. Increase the heat to medium-high and cook the caramel until it turns a deep amber (don't stir) – a bit like the colour of a penny, init.

Add the butter to the pan and swirl until it has fully melted, then add the pineapple chunks and rum and cook for 5–10 minutes, turning the chunks until they are slightly softened and glazed. Take off the heat and set aside.

SELF-SAUCY
Combine the flour and light brown sugar in a bowl and stir to mix. Beat the milk with the eggs, then add them to the flour and sugar with the crystallised ginger, melted butter and golden syrup and stir until smooth. Divide the pineapple chunks between the greased dishes. Spoon the sponge batter evenly over the pineapple, then spread to cover the fruit.

Mix the cornflour with the sugar in a bowl, then sprinkle it over the batter. Combine the 85g golden syrup and the boiling water in a heatproof jug then gently pour it over the batter in each pie dish over the back of the spoon. Bake for 25 minutes, or until a skewer comes out clean when it's inserted into the middle of the sponge.

Serve warm, ideally with a little ice cream or double cream, then you're sorted.

The Classically Steamed

Steamed Pudding
175g unsalted butter, softened, plus extra for greasing
175g soft light brown sugar
3 large eggs
75g ground almonds
grated zest of 3 unwaxed lemons
100g plain flour, plus extra for dusting
1¼ tsp baking powder
1 tsp fine sea salt
2 tbsp milk
½ tsp vanilla extract or vanilla bean paste
1 tsp almond extract
35g dried cherries
200g glacé cherries

Custard
650ml whole milk
250ml double cream
2 tsp vanilla extract or vanilla bean paste
4 large egg yolks
3 tbsp cornflour
200g soft light brown sugar

To Finish
icing sugar, for dusting
20g flaked almonds, toasted
grated zest of 1 unwaxed lemon
2 large, fresh cherries

A Bakewell-flavoured steamed pudding, a little bit of lemon zest, and that special custard. It's lit.

PUDDING

Generously grease the pudding basin with a knob of butter, then cut out a disc of baking paper the same size as the base of the basin and stick it to the bottom. Cut a large square of foil and sheet of baking paper to the same size, place them together and fold a pleat in the centre to allow your pudding to expand while cooking. If you have one of those lidded basins, that's even better.

Put the butter and sugar in the bowl of a stand mixer fitted with the beater attachment and beat until light and fluffy (or beat them in a bowl with a hand-held electric whisk). Add the eggs one at a time, beating after each addition, until well incorporated. Put the ground almonds and lemon zest in a bowl. Sift the plain flour, baking powder and salt over the almonds, then add this dry mixture to the bowl of butter, sugar and eggs and beat until incorporated. Add the milk, vanilla and almond extract to loosen the mixture.

Toss the dried cherries and 35g of the glacé cherries in a little bit of flour so there is an even distribution of cherries throughout your pudding (the flour will help prevent them all sinking to the bottom while it bakes), then quickly fold the cherries into the pudding mixture. Weirdly precise, I know.

Cut the rest of the glacé cherries in half and place them on the base of the pudding basin cut side down. Tip the pudding mixture into the basin and smooth out the surface to make it level.

Place your sheet of pleated baking paper and foil over the top of the basin and tightly secure around the edge with string, or pop the lid on.

"Get your kettle on."

turn over

Puddings

To cook the pudding, place an upturned saucer at the bottom of a large saucepan, put your pudding on top of the saucer then pour enough just-boiled water into the saucepan to reach halfway up the pudding basin. Cover the pan with a lid, bring the water back to the boil then turn down the heat to a simmer and let the pudding steam over a medium-low heat for 1½–2 hours. Have a fresh kettle of water at the ready, just in case you need to top up the water back to the halfway point.

CUSTARD

While the pudding is cooking, make the custard. Pour the milk and cream into another saucepan. Add the vanilla to the pan and warm over a low heat until just below boiling point.

While the milk and cream mixture is warming up, whisk the egg yolks with the cornflour and sugar in a separate, heatproof bowl. Slowly pour the hot milk mixture into the bowl of egg yolk and sugar mixture in a slow and steady stream, whisking constantly.

Pour the custard back into the pan and cook over a low heat for 10–15 minutes, stirring constantly with a large wooden spoon, until it thickens. It is ready when it thickly coats the back of the spoon or reaches 82°C on the food thermometer.

ASSEMBLE

Check if the pudding is ready by poking a skewer through the foil pleat and into the pudding. If it comes out clean, it's ready.

Carefully take the pudding out of the saucepan and leave it to sit for 5 minutes, then uncover it and turn it out onto your serving plate. Dust it lightly with icing sugar, sprinkle with a few toasted flaked almonds and the lemon zest, then place a pair of cherries on top. Serve with the custard.

No-Churn-but-Firm Key Lime Pie

90g white chocolate, chopped
800ml double cream
500g condensed milk
grated zest of 4 limes and
    juice of 3
300g lime curd
200g ginger biscuits, crushed

To Finish
100g ginger biscuits, roughly broken
50g white chocolate, melted
grated zest of 1 lime

I love making ice cream from scratch, starting with a custard, infusing it with flavours, cooling it, then churning it until the cow's milk comes home, but sometimes you need something a little quicker, a lot easier, but just as tasty. So here we have it: Key Lime Pie ice cream. LET'S GOOOO!

RAPID ICE CREAM
Melt the white chocolate in a heatproof bowl over a pan of barely simmering water (making sure the bottom of the bowl doesn't touch the water) or in a microwave in 20-second bursts. Let it cool.

Whisk the double cream and condensed milk in a bowl until the mixture forms soft peaks. Fold through the melted chocolate, the lime zest and lime juice gently with a metal spoon until well combined.

Pour half of the cream mixture into the loaf tin and dot half of the lime curd on top. Using a skewer or spoon, swirl the curd through the cream so it is rippled with streaks of curd, then sprinkle half the crushed ginger biscuits over the mixture. Top with the remaining cream mixture, ripple through the remaining curd, then top with the rest of the crushed ginger biscuits.

Cover with clingfilm and freeze for at least 7 hours, or ideally overnight.

FINISHING TOUCHES
Once you're ready to serve, place the roughly broken ginger biscuits on top, squiggle with melted white chocolate and sprinkle over the lime zest.

"Look at that — it's super quick! well, kinda, but remember it's easy peasy lemo... no, lime squeezy!"

The Salted Molten Dream

Spiced Caramel Bath
65ml water
230g caster sugar
85g unsalted butter
130ml double cream
½ tsp vanilla extract
 or vanilla bean paste
½ tsp ground cinnamon
¼ tsp freshly grated nutmeg
¼ tsp ground cloves
1 tsp fine sea salt

Peanut Buttered Popcorn
5 tbsp smooth peanut butter
3 tbsp maple syrup
2 tbsp coconut oil, softened
1 tsp vanilla extract
 or vanilla bean paste
½ tsp fine sea salt
60g shop-bought popcorn

Peanut Butter Lava Puds
200g unsalted butter, plus
 extra melted for greasing
cocoa powder, for dusting
300g dark chocolate (70% cocoa
 solids), broken into pieces
4 large eggs, plus 4 egg yolks
100g caster sugar
35g plain flour
100g smooth peanut butter
ice cream, to serve

This one here is pure indulgence. I'm not even going to tell you what's in it, let's just say it's the usual suspects of the indulgent crew, and then some. With this recipe there is no holding back.

CARAMEL BATH
Put the water in a saucepan, then slowly add the caster sugar, a little bit at a time, whisking constantly until it's all in the pan. Place the pan over a medium heat and let it simmer for 10–15 minutes until the sugar has turned into a deep amber colour (do not stir once the pan's over the heat).

Remove from the heat and add the butter, then return to the heat and stir until the butter is completely melted and well mixed in.

Remove from the heat again and add the double cream, vanilla, spices and salt. Mix again, return to the heat and allow to bubble for a couple of minutes. Take off the heat and set aside until ready to use.

THE CRUNCH
Preheat oven to 180°C/Fan 160°C/Gas 4 and line a large baking tray with baking paper.

Put the peanut butter, maple syrup, coconut oil, vanilla and salt in a large jug and stir until smooth. Pop the popcorn into a large bowl, pour over the peanut mixture, and stir until the popcorn is well coated. Spread the popcorn evenly over the baking tray and bake for 10 minutes until golden brown. Remove from the oven and place in a large bowl to cool. Leave the oven on.

THE LAVA PUDS
Brush the pudding moulds with a thick coating of melted butter then dust well with cocoa powder.

Melt the butter and chocolate in a heatproof bowl placed over a pan of barely simmering water (making sure the bottom of the bowl doesn't touch the water), or in the microwave in 20-second bursts, stirring occasionally. Remove and leave to cool slightly.

Whisk the eggs, egg yolks and sugar in a bowl with a hand-held electric whisk (or use a stand mixer fitted with the whisk attachment) until fluffy, doubled in size and extremely pale in colour. The mixture should leave a ribbon trail on the surface when you lift the whisk.

turn over

Puddings

Gradually whisk the melted buttery chocolate into the egg and sugar mixture. Finally, sift the flour over the mixture and gently fold it in using a large metal spoon.

Dividing the mixture between the moulds as evenly as you can, spoon about 2cm of it into each pudding mould, dot a teaspoon of peanut butter in the centre, then cover with the rest of the sponge mixture. Place the pudding moulds on a baking tray and bake for 10–12 minutes, until the sides and top appear solid.

"Cook them any longer and you may not get any ooze, any shorter you might be visiting the loo: under-baked goods are never a good thing."

ASSEMBLE
While the puddings are baking, carefully place a generous amount of salted caramel on each plate, making it look like a mini bath. Get your ice cream and popcorn at the ready.

Remove the puddings from the oven and carefully turn each one out. Place them directly in the middle of the caramel baths and finish with scoop of ice cream and the popcorn.

"This is possibly my most indulgent dessert to date."

The Fluffcake of Stackapolitan

Pancakes
300g self-raising flour
1 tsp baking powder
4 tbsp golden caster sugar
4 large eggs, beaten
2 tbsp sunflower oil
360ml whole milk
2 tsp vanilla extract
    or vanilla bean paste
2 tbsp cocoa powder
cooking spray, for frying
180g dark chocolate chips

Strawberry Daiquiri Sauce
400g fresh strawberries,
    hulled and sliced
grated zest and juice
    of 1 lime
2 tbsp caster sugar
2 tsp cornflour
2 tbsp light rum

To Finish
500g good-quality vanilla
    ice cream
6 ice-cream wafers
6 chocolate flakes

I remember the first time I came across this type of pancake. Honestly, I was shocked. They're light, they're fluffy… they could have potentially changed the pancake game forever. Here, we've got a chocolate × vanilla version with a strawberry daiquiri sauce. We call it the "stackapolitan". Let's go!

THE FLUFFIEST
Preheat oven to 150°C/Fan 130°C/Gas 2.

Sift the flour and baking powder into a bowl then add the caster sugar and mix to combine. Make a well in the centre, then add the eggs and the oil. Gradually whisk the eggs and oil into the flour, then gradually whisk in the milk followed by the vanilla.

Pour half of the pancake mixture into another bowl, and to that portion add the cocoa powder and mix it in gently.

THE LIGHTEST
Pop a frying pan (one you have a lid for) over a low heat and place 2–4 crumpet rings in the pan. Spray the pan lightly with cooking spray, and the rings too. Fill each ring no more than three-quarters full with the pancake batter, then add a few tablespoons of water to the pan. Cover the pan with a lid and cook the pancakes for 8–10 minutes. If the pancakes have little bubbles on the top and are set and cooked around the edges, they are ready!

"Low × slow wins the race."

STACK OF ALL STACKS
Turn the pancakes with a slotted spatula or a palette knife while they are still in the crumpet rings – you have to do this quickly, because at this point they're not entirely cooked. Cook for a further 2 minutes, then transfer to a heatproof plate, remove the crumpet rings and keep the pancakes warm in the oven while you cook the remaining batter, adding more water to the pan if necessary (you need the water to create steam, which helps the pancakes cook). You should get 6 vanilla pancakes and 6 chocolate pancakes.

Repeat the same process with the chocolate pancakes, adding a sprinkle of the chocolate chips to each crumpet ring just before you flip them over.

Puddings

turn over

THE STRAWBERRY SAUCIEST
Put the strawberries, lime juice and zest, and sugar in the bowl of a food-processor and blitz to a purée (basically a liquid).

Put the strawberry purée, cornflour and rum in a saucepan and whisk to get rid of any lumps, then place over a medium heat and cook, stirring occasionally, for 5–10 minutes until it thickens. Take the sauce off the heat, leave to cool, then chill in the fridge until ready to serve.

THE STACKAPOLITAN
For each serving, stack a chocolate pancake on top of a vanilla pancake, top with a scoop of ice cream, then finish with a wafer and flake. Finally, drizzle with the strawberry sauce – we are talking about generous drizzles here.

TIP
If you prefer, you can blitz the pancake ingredients in a blender or food-processor until the batter is super smooth (before flavouring half the batter with cocoa powder). Just make sure all your dry ingredients are sifted first.

Puddings

Caramel Soft-Serve

Rum Caramel
65ml water
230g caster sugar
90g unsalted butter
150ml double cream
2 tbsp rum (optional)
1 tsp vanilla extract
    or vanilla bean paste

Rapid Ice Cream
550ml double cream
200g condensed milk
1 tbsp vanilla extract
    or vanilla bean paste

Topping × Filling
200g smooth peanut butter
200g dry roasted peanuts
100g salted mini pretzels,
    roughly crushed

To Finish
50g dry roasted peanuts
50g salted large pretzels

If you know, you know. Caramel, peanuts, pretzels: it's a must, it's a necessity, it's a way of life. Again, this is a no-churn ice cream, salted but with a sweet vibe. All you need is a few cones to serve it in and you're sorted. Get started the day before.

RUM CARAMEL

Put the water in a saucepan, then gradually add the caster sugar, stirring to combine it evenly with the water. Place the pan over a medium heat and heat for about 10 minutes until the sugar has dissolved to a caramel and turned a deep amber colour (don't stir once the pan is over the heat).

Take the pan off the heat, add the butter, then return to the heat and stir until the butter has completely melted and is well mixed in.

Remove from the heat again, add the double cream, rum (if using) and vanilla and mix again. Return to the heat for a few more seconds, then pour into a heatproof bowl and set aside.

PEANUT BUTTER × RAPID ICE CREAM

Put the smooth peanut butter in a bowl and loosen it by warming it in the microwave in three or four 30-second bursts, stirring each time (or warm it in a pan over a low heat).

To make the ice cream mixture, whisk the double cream, condensed milk and vanilla together in a bowl until the mixture forms soft peaks. Fold through 2 tablespoons of the caramel.

Pour half of the ice cream mixture into the loaf tin and dot half of the loosened peanut butter on top. Use a skewer or spoon to swirl the peanut butter through the ice cream mixture then sprinkle half the nuts and pretzels over the mixture. Repeat the process with the remaining ice cream mixture, peanut butter, nuts and pretzels. Cover with clingfilm and freeze for at least 7 hours, or ideally overnight.

FINISHING TOUCHES

Once you're ready to serve, top off with some large pretzels, some more of those nuts, and generous squiggles of the caramel.

"Go on: give yourself 2 hefty scoops. Ahhh, and maybe one pretzel... yes, a few nuts as well. FINE, squiggle that caramel. LOVE IT."

Soft–Serve Goat

Ice Cream
100g soft goat's cheese
6 large egg yolks
450ml whole milk
450ml double cream
220g runny honey
1 tsp ground cardamom
2 vanilla pods, split lengthways
250g fig jam
dark chocolate shavings,
    to serve (optional)

There's a trend for making traditional sweet treats savoury. Especially with ice cream. This one has bougie flavours: goat's cheese, fig and honey. Yes, in an ice cream, but trust me, when you try it you'll be hooked. Make the custard at least a day before you want to serve the ice cream.

DAY I

CUSTARD

Pop the cheese in a large bowl, give it a good whisk for a minute or so until smooth, then set aside. Place a fine sieve over the bowl.

Whisk the egg yolks in a separate, heatproof bowl.

Put the milk, cream, honey and ground cardamom in a large saucepan. Scrape the seeds from the vanilla pods and add the seeds and the pods to the pan. Warm over a low heat, but do not allow the milk to simmer or boil as this could cause the honey to curdle the milk.

Slowly pour the warm milk into the bowl of egg yolks, whisking constantly.

Pour the custard back into the pan and cook over a low heat for 10–15 minutes, stirring constantly with a wooden spoon, until it thickens. If it reads 75°C on a thermometer – it should coat the back of a wooden spoon – you're good to go.

Strain the custard through the sieve over the bowl of goat's cheese and whisk until the goat's cheese is thoroughly combined with the custard. Place a sheet of clingfilm over the surface of the custard, allow the custard to cool completely, then place in the fridge to chill overnight.

DAY II

CHURN THAT CHEESE

Churn the custard in an ice-cream machine according to the manufacturer's instructions. Once it's churned, pop it in a freezer-proof container. Dot your fig jam over the ice cream and swirl it with a spoon to give the ice cream a ripple effect. Put the container back in the freezer, covered with a lid, to freeze until solid.

ASSEMBLE

About 10 minutes before serving, remove the ice cream from the freezer so it softens slightly. When ready to serve, top each scoop with a few dark chocolate shavings (if you like) and... BOOM.

Cakes, Bakes, Biscuits

05

Pastel de Baklava

Pimped Pastry
3 tsp ground cinnamon
1 tsp ground cardamom
grated zest of 4 unwaxed lemons
2 x 500g blocks all-butter
    puff pastry
plain flour, for dusting
knob of unsalted butter, melted
    (optional), plus extra for greasing
80g ground pistachios, to finish

Custard
250ml whole milk
250ml double cream
1 tsp vanilla extract
    or vanilla bean paste
1 tsp orange blossom extract
8 large egg yolks
100g golden caster sugar
1 tbsp cornflour

There is a massive Turkish community where I live, and some wicked Turkish restaurants. Here's a secret: if you are a regular customer, or they like you, they will always give you a square of baklava when you've finished your meal. Some of my pals say it's too sweet, so I eat their piece, but one thing we all agree on is that the flavour of the baklava itself is insane and super tasty. Combining that with my love for Portuguese tarts… it's a winner.

PIMPED PASTRY
Preheat oven to 210°C/Fan 190°C/Gas 6–7 and lightly grease the muffin tray.

Combine the ground cinnamon, cardamom and lemon zest in a small bowl.

Roll out the first block of the pastry a little on a lightly floured surface.

Place it on a large baking sheet and evenly sprinkle over half the spices and keep rolling, pressing the cinnamon, cardamom and lemon zest into the pastry, until you have a rectangle measuring about 20 x 50cm that's about 5mm thick. Cover the pastry with clingfilm and chill in the fridge (on the tray) for 30 minutes. Repeat the process with the second block of pastry.

CUSTARD
Put the milk and cream into a medium saucepan with the vanilla and orange blossom extract. Warm over a low heat until just below boiling point.

Meanwhile, whisk the egg yolks, sugar and cornflour together in a bowl and mix until smooth.

Pour a little of the warm milk mixture into the egg yolk mixture, whisking constantly, then gently, in a steady stream, whisk in the rest of the warm milk mixture until it is well combined. Transfer to a jug and set aside.

turn over

CHOMP × **FILL** × **BAKE**

Take one of the pieces of chilled pastry from the fridge and cut out 6–9 discs using the round cutter. Put the discs into the holes in the greased muffin tray. Press gently into the bases and up the sides of each hole to form a cup. Repeat with the second batch of pimped pastry.

Pour the custard filling in the pastry cases to 1cm below the top of each case. Bake for 20–22 minutes, until the custard tarts are set with a crisp pastry edge and a slightly caramelised custard.

Remove from the oven and allow to cool for 5 minutes in the muffin tray, then pop out each tart and place on a wire rack.

While the tarts are still slightly warm, roll the pastry edge of each tart in ground pistachios (brush the edges with a little melted butter to help the nuts stick, if necessary). Serve warm or at room temperature.

"Oi oi, pastel de baklava."

Pimp That Bar

Biscuit Base
70g unsalted butter, plus
　　extra for greasing
240g shortbread biscuits, crushed

Cheese Filling
400g full-fat cream cheese
3 tbsp dulce de leche
120g golden caster sugar
1 tbsp plain flour
160g soured cream
½ tsp vanilla extract
　　or vanilla bean paste
2 large eggs

Miso × Macadamia Caramel Layer
90ml double cream
½ tsp vanilla extract
　　or vanilla bean paste
185g caster sugar
30g liquid glucose
150g salted butter,
　　softened
2 tbsp white miso paste
150g unsalted macadamia
　　nuts, roughly chopped

Chocolate Ganache
400g milk chocolate, chopped
400ml double cream

This bake is inspired by one of my favourite chocolate bars of all time. I have made a few versions of this bake, messing around with different sizes and flavour combinations, and ended up with four layers and loads of textures – it's going to be huge!

THE BASE

Preheat oven to 180°C/Fan 160°C/Gas 4. Grease the loaf tin and, as smoothly as possible, line the base and sides with clingfilm.

Put the butter in a saucepan and heat until it's just melted. Put the crushed shortbread biscuits into a bowl and pour over the melted butter, stirring at the same time, until well combined.

Tip the shortbread mixture into the lined tin and gently press it into the base until it's well compacted. Bake for 15 minutes, then reduce the oven temperature to 150°C/Fan 130°C/Gas 2.

THE CHEESE FILLING

Put the cream cheese in a large bowl with the dulce de leche and golden caster sugar and beat with a hand-held electric whisk or in the bowl of a stand mixer until creamy. Add the flour, soured cream and vanilla, beat to combine, then add the eggs one at a time, beating between each addition until fully incorporated. Pour the filling on top of the baked biscuit base and bake for 35–40 minutes. It should still have a cheeky little wobble in the middle.

Once the cheesecake is baked, switch off the heat and allow it to cool in the oven, leaving the oven door ajar for 30 minutes minimum.

Place the cheesecake in the fridge to chill for a couple hours, or ideally overnight.

MISO CARAMEL

Put a baking tray in the freezer.

Put the cream and vanilla in a saucepan and bring to the boil, then take off the heat.

Heat an empty saucepan over a medium heat. When it is hot, add one-third of the sugar with the liquid glucose, reduce the heat to low and heat gently for about 10 minutes until it forms a light caramel and the sugar crystals have dissolved.

turn over

Stir in the remaining sugar and continue to cook over a medium heat until you get an amber caramel – this will take about 15 minutes.

Slowly add the warm cream to the caramel, mix well, then take off the heat and add small chunks of butter at a time. Once all the butter is melted, add the miso paste and stir to combine.

Place the pan back over a medium heat and bring the caramel up to a final temperature of 120°C (using a sugar thermometer to test it).

Pour the caramel onto the frozen baking tray and give it a good stir – this will help with cooling process – then fold the nuts into the caramel. Pour the caramel into a disposable piping bag while it's still warm, then evenly distribute the caramel over the cheesecake layer. Place the loaf tin in the freezer for 30–40 minutes until the caramel is set to touch.

GANACHE
Place the milk chocolate in a large heatproof bowl. Bring the cream to a gentle simmer in a pan, then pour it over the chocolate and whisk until the chocolate has melted and the mixture is smooth.

ASSEMBLE
Gently pull the "chocolate bar" out of the loaf tin and peel off the clingfilm. Place on a display board.

Pour the milk chocolate ganache over the bar, using a small palette knife to smooth it and making sure you cover the top and sides. Finally, give the top of the bar a few classic swooshes with your palette knife. Pop it in the fridge for a couple of hours for it to firm up, then slice into portions.

"My favourite."

21

Brown Butter Sponge
750g unsalted butter, cubed, plus extra for greasing
500g golden caster sugar
8 large eggs
375g self-raising flour
125g ground almonds
2 tsp baking powder
2 tsp ground mixed spice
120ml whole milk
1 tsp vanilla extract or vanilla bean paste
7 ripe peaches (about 1kg), peeled, halved, stoned and diced

Bacon Crumble
2 tsp dark spiced rum
150g soft light brown sugar
10 rashers smoked streaky bacon
150g plain flour
125g unsalted butter, cold, diced
60g light muscovado sugar
30g pecans, roughly chopped

Blue-cheese Buttercream
600g unsalted butter, softened
75–100g dolcelatte cheese
1.3kg icing sugar, sifted
5–8 tbsp whole milk

Yup, I gave you the "19" in my first book. By the time this book comes out I'll be 22, but I did make my own birthday cake for my 21st birthday. Making my own meant I could do what I wanted and I ended up with one of my best "wrong but so right" flavour combinations to date. This amazing, salty-sweet, brown-butter peach cake not only has a bacon pecan crumble, but also blue-cheese buttercream. Trust me – it works. This is the perfect cake to celebrate someone special who doesn't play by the rules. I've given you the quantities for a cake that's half the size of my actual birthday cake, but if you wanna take it up a level, double all the ingredients and make it an absolute tower of a cake.

BROWN BUTTER × BAKE YOUR SPONGE
Place the butter in a large heavy-based saucepan over a medium-high heat. Stir as the butter melts then cook for about 15 minutes, until the milk solids have separated from the fat and almost burnt, and the fat becomes a dark amber–brown colour.

Pour the butter into a heatproof container and leave it to cool, then chill for 15–20 minutes in the fridge until solidified.

Preheat oven to 180°C/Fan 160°C/Gas 4 and grease and line the base and sides of the cake tins.

Measure out 500g of the solidified brown butter and place it in a large bowl with the caster sugar. Beat with a hand-held electric whisk or in a stand mixer until light and fluffy, then add the eggs one at a time, beating well after each addition, until they are fully incorporated. If the mixture starts to curdle, add a couple of tablespoons of the flour and that should help bring it back together.

Combine the self-raising flour, ground almonds, baking powder and mixed spice in a separate bowl, then gradually add the dry mixture to the wet mixture one third at a time, scraping down the sides of the bowl to make sure everything is well mixed. Loosen the mixture with the milk, then add the vanilla and stir to combine. Fold in the diced peaches.

Divide the mixture equally between the prepared tins and bake for 25–30 minutes, or until a skewer inserted into the centre of each cake comes out clean. Remove from the oven and leave to cool in the tins for 5 minutes, then turn out onto a wire rack to cool completely. (If you don't have 4 cake tins, weigh the cake batter and divide it by the number of tins you have and bake in batches... maths is my strong point but I can't help you with this one.)

BACON CRUMBLY TASTY BITS

Increase the oven temperature to 190°C/Fan 170°C/Gas 5 and line a baking tray with foil.

Combine the rum and the light brown sugar in a bowl. Add the bacon rashers to the bowl and turn them and rub them in the mixture until well coated. Place the rashers on the foil-lined baking tray and cook in the oven for 10 minutes on one side, then flip them and cook for a further 5 minutes, until crisp. Remove from the oven, allow to cool, then chop into small pieces. Set aside. Reduce the oven temperature to 180°C/Fan 160°C/Gas 4.

Put the flour and butter in a food-processor and pulse until the mixture resembles coarse breadcrumbs (or rub the butter into the flour with your fingertips). Stir in the muscovado sugar and chopped pecans and sprinkle the mixture over an unlined baking tray. Bake for 10–15 minutes, until the crumble is golden brown and moves when you shake the tray from side to side. Remove from the oven and set aside.

GO BLUE

Make the blue-cheese buttercream. Use a wooden spoon to beat together the butter and the dolcelatte in a bowl for 5–8 minutes until light and fluffy. (Alternatively, you can do this in a stand mixer fitted with the beater attachment.) Add half the icing sugar to the butter mixture and beat well to combine. Repeat with the other half of icing sugar. Add enough milk to loosen the mixture and beat again until light and fluffy.

ASSEMBLE

Once the cakes have cooled, using a cake leveller or a sharp knife, trim the top of all the cakes so they are level. Spread a small amount of buttercream on a cake board and top with the first sponge. Place the cake board on the cake-decorating turntable.

Fill the piping bag with the buttercream. In a bowl, combine the crumble with the crispy bacon pieces. Snip the end of the piping bag and pipe a thin, even layer of buttercream on top of the first sponge, while rotating the turntable, then sprinkle over about one fifth of the bacon crumble. Repeat for all the sponges, reserving some bacon crumble for decoration and finishing with the final sponge placed face down on top of the stack.

Coat the outside of the stacked cake with a thin layer of buttercream (a palette knife and cake scraper will help you here). Place in the fridge for at least 1 hour to set.

Remove the cake from the fridge and apply another layer of buttercream around the outside of the cake, reserving some buttercream for decoration. Using a small offset palette knife, start at the bottom of the cake and gently press the tip of your palette knife into the buttercream, rotating at the same time. Gradually move up and around the cake to create a ripple effect.

Pipe a border of buttercream around the top edge of the cake and sprinkle over some of the reserved bacon crumble. Press a ring of crumble around the bottom edge of the cake to finish.

Apple × Peanut Butter S'more Cookies

Cookies
250g unsalted butter, softened
70g soft light brown sugar
70g light muscovado sugar
100g smooth peanut butter
1 large egg yolk
2 tsp vanilla extract
    or vanilla bean paste
300g plain flour
1 tsp fine sea salt
¼ tsp bicarbonate of soda
100g peanuts, crushed
2 tbsp icing sugar, to decorate

Apple Curd
80g unsalted butter
80ml apple juice
2 large eggs, plus 2 egg yolks
250g caster sugar
2 tsp cornflour

Filling
1 x 213g tub marshmallow fluff
½ tsp ground cinnamon

You can make simple bakes amazing with a few clever twists. This recipe shows this concept off perfectly and includes some of my favourite flavours, combining sweet and salty with a simple cookie, an easy apple curd and cinnamon-spiced marshmallow. Absolutely tasty!

DOUGH
Preheat oven to 180°C/Fan 160°C/Gas 4 and line two baking trays with baking paper.

Cream the butter, both sugars and the peanut butter in a large bowl until light and fluffy, using an electric hand-held mixer or stand mixer fitted with the beater attachment, then add the egg yolk and vanilla and mix again.

Sift the flour, salt and bicarbonate of soda into a separate bowl, then add the flour mixture to the butter mixture and beat to combine. Just before the cookie mix comes together, chuck in those nuts.

Using the hinged ice-cream scoop, place 16 portions of the cookie dough on the lined baking trays, spacing them out to allow for spreading, and press them down gently to flatten the bottom. Bake for 12–15 minutes, until golden, then remove from the oven, leave to cool slightly and firm up, then transfer to a wire rack to cool.

CURD
While the cookies are in the oven, make the apple curd. Put the butter and apple juice in a small, heavy-based pan, place over a low heat and warm through for a minute or so until the butter has melted.

Meanwhile, whisk the whole eggs, yolks, caster sugar and cornflour in a bowl until completely smooth.

Whisk the egg mixture into the pan with the melted butter gradually, then cook, stirring, for 5–8 minutes, until the curd is thick and glossy. Remove from the heat and pour into a deep baking tray to cool.

turn over

ASSEMBLE

Once both the cookies and curd are cool, spoon the curd into a disposable piping bag.

Spoon the marshmallow fluff into a piping bag fitted with a star nozzle.

Turn one cookie upside down and pipe marshmallow around the edge of the flat side. Fill the centre with a little curd using the piping bag (1–2 teaspoonfuls). Sprinkle the filling with cinnamon. Use a kitchen blowtorch to carefully colour the marshmallow, if you wish. Place another cookie on top, flat side downwards, to sandwich the filling.

Repeat with the remaining cookies, then dust the cookies with icing sugar and serve immediately.

"I swear, if you close your eyes, it tastes like an apple crumble."

WTB (White Chocolate × Tahini × Blackberry) Slicer

White Chocolate Sponge
500g unsalted butter,
 plus extra for greasing
200g white chocolate, broken
 into chunks
500g golden caster sugar
8 large eggs
500g self-raising flour
1 tsp vanilla extract
 or vanilla bean paste

Blackberry Filling
2 tbsp cornflour
45ml water, plus 4 tbsp
 for the cornflour
450g frozen or fresh blackberries
grated zest and juice
 of 1 unwaxed lemon
3 tbsp runny honey
3 tbsp golden caster sugar

White Chocolate Ganache
125ml double cream
300g white chocolate,
 broken into pieces

Tahini Buttercream
300g unsalted butter, softened
60g tahini
650g icing sugar
4–5 tbsp whole milk
1 tsp vanilla extract
 or vanilla bean paste

Sesame Praline
300g caster sugar
4 tbsp water
80g sesame seeds

To Finish
100g white chocolate,
 broken into pieces
100g "pretty" blackberries

Honestly, this is one of my favourite flavour combinations, and the slices are really generous. I mean, you can halve it but it's cake and we don't have time for that (lol). In my last book I gave you the "WLB" (white chocolate × lemon × blueberry), this year you get the big "WTB". It's super tasty, and well worth the effort.

BAKE
Preheat oven to 180°C/Fan 160°C/Gas 4. Grease the two baking tins and line the base and sides with baking paper.

Put the butter and white chocolate in a heatproof bowl over a pan of barely simmering water (making sure the bottom of the bowl doesn't touch the water) and let them melt, stirring occasionally. Alternatively, melt in the microwave in 20-second bursts, stirring. Leave it to cool for a couple of minutes.

Using a hand-held electric mixer or stand mixer, beat the golden caster sugar into the white chocolate, then add the eggs one by one, beating between each addition. Once the eggs are fully incorporated, fold in the flour and vanilla.

Divide the cake mixture between the two baking tins, making sure the mixture is spread evenly so it bakes correctly. Bake for 25–30 minutes, until the centres of the cakes spring back when you gently press them. Remove from the oven and place both trays on a wire rack to cool. While they're cooling…

"Crack on with your fillings."

BLACKBERRY FILLING
Mix the cornflour in a small bowl with the 4 tablespoons of water, then put it in a medium saucepan with all the remaining blackberry filling ingredients. Place over a medium-low heat and cook for 10–15 minutes, stirring occasionally, until it becomes a thick, glossy, sweet, sour fruity thing. Pour the cooked fruit into a heatproof bowl and leave to cool.

WHITE CHOCOLATE GANACHE
Pour the double cream into a saucepan and heat it gently. In the meantime, put the chocolate into a heatproof bowl. Once the cream is just simmering, pour it over the chocolate and leave it to melt for a couple of minutes, then stir until glossy and smooth. Set aside.

turn over

TAHINI BUTTERCREAM
Cream your butter and tahini in a bowl with a hand-held electric whisk, or using a stand mixer, until light and fluffy, and beige in colour. Sift your icing sugar into a separate bowl. Add the icing sugar to the butter and tahini mixture in two batches. Your buttercream will be stiff, so to loosen it add the milk, then add the vanilla.

SESAME PRALINE
Put the caster sugar and water in a large heavy-based saucepan, place over a medium-high heat and heat until the sugar crystals have dissolved and it has developed a deep amber colour – swirling the pan will help evenly distribute the sugar (do not stir). Remove from the heat, tip in your sesame seeds, stir and pour onto a silicone mat or sheet of baking paper and leave to set.

FRESH TRIM
Carefully remove both sponge layers from the tins. Level your cakes using a serrated knife or a cake leveller. Place the cake layers on top of each other and, using a sharp knife and a ruler, trim the edges of the cakes so both the cakes are same width and length.

Cut the cakes in half lengthways to make 4 strips of white chocolate sponge.

"Don't forget to remove the baking paper from the cakes."

Beat the white chocolate ganache with a hand-held electric whisk until pale and fluffy.

ASSEMBLE
Fill each of the two piping bags with the tahini buttercream and the white chocolate ganache.

Spread a thin a layer of buttercream onto a cake board, then place that onto a turntable if you have one.

Place your first layer of sponge on top of the board, then use the buttercream to create a border around the top of the cake. Now create another border with the white chocolate ganache, just inside the buttercream border. Finally, fill the centre with the blackberry mixture.

Repeat this process twice more, then place the final layer of sponge upside down on top and gently press it down. Coat your cake all over with a thin layer of buttercream (this is to lock in the crumbs), then place in the fridge for at least 1 hour to set.

TO FINISH
Melt the white chocolate in a heatproof bowl placed over a pan of barely simmering water (making sure the bottom of the bowl doesn't touch the water).

Remove the cake from the fridge and squiggle the melted white chocolate in one direction over the cake with a spoon, then in another direction, for a criss-cross effect.

Pipe buttercream "kisses" down the middle of the cake lengthways, topping each one with a single fresh blackberry. Finally, place shards of sesame praline on top of the cake and around the sides.

What Came First, the Egg or the Lemon?

Honey Soak
175g runny honey
50ml water
2 tbsp fresh lemon juice

Lemon × Herby Curd
8 large unwaxed lemons
a couple of sprigs of thyme
100g unsalted butter
200g caster sugar
3 large eggs, beaten
3 tbsp runny honey

Sponge
500g unsalted butter, softened
500g golden caster sugar
8 large eggs
1 tbsp vanilla extract
   or vanilla bean paste
500g self-raising flour
a couple of sprigs of thyme,
   leaves picked
1 tsp baking powder
grated zest of 4 unwaxed lemons
120ml whole milk

Herby Curd Buttercream
600g unsalted butter, softened
1.3kg icing sugar
7 tbsp whole milk
5 tbsp Lemon × Herby Curd
   (see above)
1 tsp vanilla extract
   or vanilla bean paste

Filling
200g ginger biscuits,
   roughly chopped
4 shop-bought meringue nests,
   roughly crushed

This cake is simply a celebration of the humble lemon and meringue. These two flavours work SOOO well together you can put them in almost everything. Yes, almost everything. Here, it's a layered cake! WHOOOOOPPPP!

HONEY SOAK

Put the honey, water and lemon juice in a small saucepan and place over a medium heat. Heat, stirring occasionally, and allow to boil until it has reduced by a quarter. Remove from the heat and set aside to cool.

LEMON × HERB CURD

Grate the zest from 4 of the lemons then juice all the lemons. Put the lemon zest, lemon juice and thyme into a large saucepan with the butter and caster sugar and place over a low heat, stirring, until the sugar has dissolved and the butter has melted. Take the pan off the heat for a couple of minutes – you do not want to add the eggs while the mixture is too hot.

Once it's slightly cool, add the beaten eggs, return to the heat and cook over a low heat for 5 minutes, whisking constantly, until the curd is thick, gloopy and glossy. Pass the curd through a sieve into a heatproof bowl, stir in the honey and allow to cool.

CAKE

Preheat oven to 180°C/Fan 160°C/Gas 4. Grease the cake tins and line the bases and sides with baking paper.

Using a hand-held electric whisk, or a stand mixer fitted with the beater attachment, cream together the butter and sugar until light and fluffy.

Add the eggs one at a time, beating well after each addition. If the mixture seems like it's going to curdle, pop in a few tablespoons of the flour to help bring it back together. Finally, combine the vanilla, flour, thyme leaves, baking powder and lemon zest in a bowl, then fold them in to the wet mixture (or mix in on a very low speed on your stand mixer), followed by the milk.

Divide the cake mixture equally between the lined tins and bake for 30 minutes, or until a skewer inserted into the middle of the cakes comes out clean. Remove from the oven and allow the cakes to cool on a wire rack in the tins for 5 minutes before turning them out to cool fully.

turn over for more ingredients

Marshy Mellow Topping
3 large egg whites
5 tbsp golden syrup
200g caster sugar
½ tsp cream of tartar
1 tsp fine sea salt
2 tbsp water
1½ tsp vanilla extract
   or vanilla bean paste
1 tsp ground cinnamon

BUTTERCREAM

Beat the butter with a hand-held electric whisk or your stand mixer until light and pale. Sift the icing sugar into a separate bowl, then add it to the butter in three stages and beat for a couple more minutes, scraping down the sides of the bowl from time to time. Add the milk, curd and vanilla to loosen the buttercream.

ASSEMBLE I

Once the cakes have cooled, using a cake leveller or a sharp knife, trim the top of all the cakes so they are level. Using a pastry brush, brush the surface of the cakes with the honey soak.

Using a board slightly bigger than your sponges, spread a small amount of buttercream on it and place your first layer of sponge onto it, then place the board on top of the turntable.

Spoon the buttercream into a disposable piping bag, snip the end and create a border around the first layer of cake, leaving an 8cm circle in the middle. Fill that circle with a quarter of the remaining curd, sprinkle over a third of the ginger biscuits and a third of the crushed meringues. Cover with a second layer of sponge and repeat the process with the same quantities of the curd, ginger biscuits and meringues, and again with the third. Place the final sponge face down on top of the stack.

Coat the stacked cake all over with a thin layer of buttercream (a palette knife and cake scraper will make this easier) and add a thin layer of buttercream to the top of the cake. Place in the fridge for at least 1 hour to set.

MARSHY MELLOW

Combine the egg whites, golden syrup, caster sugar, cream of tartar, salt and water in a heatproof bowl over a pan of barely simmering water (make sure the bottom of the bowl isn't touching the water). Beat using a hand-held electric whisk for 10–15 minutes until the mixture forms stiff peaks, then remove the bowl from the saucepan and add the vanilla and cinnamon. Fold them in gently, leave to cool, then spoon into the piping bag fitted with the nozzle.

ASSEMBLE II

Remove the cake from the fridge and apply the rest of the buttercream around the side and on top of the cake. Using the miniature offset palette knife, starting from the bottom of the cake gently press the tip sideways into the cake while you move it up and around the cake, turning the turntable at the same time, to create a rippled effect.

Keeping the cake on the turntable, pipe a spiral of marshmallow topping around the top of the cake, leaving an 8cm circle in the middle. Spoon the remaining extra curd into the circle and spread it out evenly.

Finally, give that marshmallow topping a cheeky dose of heat from the blowtorch.

Rice Pudding Holders

Cakes, Bakes, Biscuits

Rice Pudding Mix
1 x 400g tin rice pudding
¼ tsp freshly grated nutmeg

Nostalgic Base
10 Jammy Dodgers

Rice Pudding Sponge
330g unsalted butter, softened,
    plus extra for greasing
330g golden caster sugar
6 large eggs
330g self-raising flour,
    plus extra for dusting
1½ tsp baking powder
6 tbsp reduced rice pudding
    mix (see above)
1½ tsp vanilla extract
    or vanilla bean paste
150g raspberry jam
10g freeze-dried raspberries,
    to serve
ground cinnamon, for dusting
¼ tsp freshly grated nutmeg

Rice Pudding Buttercream
300g unsalted butter, softened
600g icing sugar, sifted
8 tbsp reduced rice pudding
    mix (see above)
1 tsp vanilla extract
    or vanilla bean paste

You either love or hate rice pudding, but I tell you what, after you've tried this recipe, rice pudding will never seem the same again. So, if you find a neglected tin of rice pudding at the back of your cupboard, you know what to do. OOOOOO, and we've got a surprise at the bottom as well. It's mad! I mean, if you don't like these then… actually, there's no choice, lol. ENJOY :D

RICE PUDDING MIX

Pour the tinned rice pudding into a saucepan, add the nutmeg and simmer over a low heat for 10–15 minutes, until reduced by half, stirring occasionally to avoid the rice pudding sticking to the bottom of the pan. Set aside.

Grease the base and sides of your mini pudding moulds generously with butter, dust them with flour, then line the base with a circle of baking paper. Do this stage properly – trust me, it's worth it. Place one biscuit directly in the centre of each pudding mould. Place the moulds on two baking trays (5 on each) and leave to the side.

RICE PUDDING SPONGE

Preheat oven to 180°C/Fan 160°C/Gas 4.

Cream the butter and golden caster sugar in the bowl of a stand mixer fitted with the beater attachment (or using a hand-held electric whisk) until light and fluffy. Add the eggs one at a time, mixing well between each addition.

Sift the flour and baking powder into a separate bowl, then with the mixer on a slow speed, add the flour mixture. When completely combined, add the 6 tablespoons of rice pudding mix and the vanilla.

Evenly divide the mixture between the pudding moulds, then top each filled tin with a tablespoon of jam. Using a skewer, gently swirl the jam through the sponge mixture to create a marble effect on the top of each cake. Place the remaining jam in the small disposable piping bag.

turn over

Bake the sponges for 25 minutes, or until a skewer inserted into the centres comes out clean. Remove from the oven and allow to cool on the baking trays for 5 minutes then place on a wire rack. As soon as the moulds are cool enough to touch, encourage the cakes to pop out by flipping them upside down. If they don't come out easily, just run a palette knife around the edge of each pudding that's stuck and try again – that should do the trick.

RICE PUDDING BUTTERCREAM

Cream the butter in the bowl of the stand mixer or with a hand-held electric whisk on medium-high speed until light and pale. Add the icing sugar, a third at a time, and mix until fully combined, then add the 8 tablespoons of rice pudding mix and the vanilla. Mix for a couple more minutes until completely combined. Transfer the buttercream mixture to the piping bag fitted with the nozzle. Place the remaining reduced rice pudding mix in the large disposable piping bag.

ASSEMBLE

Flip all the puddings over so they are sitting with the bigger face up. Using an apple corer, take out the centre of each mini cake to about three-quarters of the way down. Cut 5mm off the tip of the rice-pudding piping bag and fill the hole in each cake with the rice pudding.

Pipe two rings of buttercream on top of each other, around the top of each cupcake, to create a buttercream bowl. Fill up each bowl with the remaining reduced rice pudding. Cut the smallest hole possible in the end of the jam piping bag and squeeze a little dot of raspberry jam on top of each cake, then sprinkle with freeze-dried raspberries and a little cinnamon and nutmeg.

Makes 10   Skill Level: light work   You will need two 30 x 20cm deep
baking trays and a 6cm square
cookie cutter

The Tipsy Malty Sarnie

Malty Irish Ice Cream
200g barley malt syrup
3 tbsp Irish cream liqueur
1.5 litres vanilla ice cream

Hazelnut Shortbread
340g unsalted butter, softened
165g golden caster sugar
340g plain flour, plus
    extra for dusting
165g cornflour
200g blanched hazelnuts,
    roughly chopped
1 tbsp vanilla extract
    or vanilla bean paste

Dipping Chocolate × Decoration
400g white chocolate (30% cocoa
    solids), broken into pieces
500g malted-middle,
    choc-coated chocolates

One of the main things I love about ice-cream sandwiches is that they're a texture playground. This recipe is banging: there's shortbread to keep the crunch, a quick-hack ice-cream that's a super chilling temperature change, not to mention the dipped chocolate edges and all those toppings. You could even dip it with… I'll tell you that part later.

MALTY IRISH ICE CREAM
Line one of the deep baking trays with baking paper.

Put the malt syrup and Irish cream liqueur in a small saucepan over a low heat and heat for 2–3 minutes until loosened, then remove from the heat and set aside.

Blitz the ice cream in a food-processor until smooth, then leave the motor running and pour the malt syrup through the feeding tube, continuing to mix until combined.

Spread the ice cream out evenly on one of the lined deep baking trays and place it in the freezer for 1 hour.

Wash the food-processor bowl and blade.

SHORTBREAD
Make the shortbread. Cream the butter and sugar together in the bowl of a stand mixer until light and fluffy, then add the plain flour and cornflour, followed by the chopped hazelnuts and vanilla. Mix until the dough is just coming together. Wrap it in clingfilm and chill for 20 minutes.

Preheat oven to 170°C/Fan 150°C/Gas 3 and line two baking trays with baking paper.

Place the chilled dough on a lightly floured surface and knead it gently for 1 minute, then roll it out to a thickness of 1cm. Using the square cookie cutter, cut out 20 squares, re-rolling the trimmings as necessary, and place them on the two lined baking trays.

Place the trays in the freezer for 5–10 minutes, then place them in the oven to bake for 8–10 minutes, until the shortbread is pale golden. Remove from the oven and leave to firm up on the baking trays for 5 minutes, then place on a wire rack to cool fully.

turn over

Cakes, Bakes, Biscuits

ASSEMBLE

Remove the ice cream from the freezer once set and use the cookie cutter again to cut out 10 ice-cream squares. (Alternatively, mark the squares with the cutter and use a knife to cut through the ice cream.) Put the second, deep baking tray in the freezer and as you cut out each ice-cream square, place it straight on the tray until you have 10 squares in total.

Sandwich the ice-cream squares between two pieces of shortbread, then put the ice-cream sandwiches back in the freezer for 5–10 minutes while you melt the chocolate for dipping and get your decorations sorted.

DIP × COAT

Melt the white chocolate in a heatproof bowl over a pan of barely simmering water (making sure the bowl doesn't touch the water), or in a microwave in 20-second bursts, stirring occasionally.

Place the malted-middle, choc-coated chocolates in a food-processor and blitz until crushed into irregular pieces.

Dip one side of each ice-cream sandwich in the melted chocolate, going halfway up, then dip the side that's completely covered in white chocolate in the crushed chocolates. Enjoy straight away, or wrap the sandwiches in baking paper and clingfilm and freeze for up to a month.

TIPS

Switch it up if you want to. You can use different treats to coat the sandwiches, and dip and coat them all over so that the ice cream is completely hidden on all sides.

If you don't fancy the Irish liqueur, just give it a miss – the sandwich still tastes just as good!

"For me, the best way to eat these is to leave them to freeze for a couple of hours, then make a hot chocolate, sit on the sofa watching your favourite baking/cooking show (cough cough, hint), then dip a corner of the ice-cream sandwich into the mug. Thank me later."

Cupboard Cookies

Cookies
250g unsalted butter, softened
70g soft light brown sugar
70g caster sugar
2 tsp vanilla extract
    or vanilla bean paste
2 large eggs
300g plain flour
1 tsp fine sea salt
¼ tsp bicarbonate of soda

Cupboard Treats
100g sweet 'n' salty popcorn
240g crispy M & Ms,
    roughly chopped
150g pretzels, roughly chopped

Alright… it's pretty fair to say we all have those snacks in our cupboard that we get out probably once or twice a year then put back into hibernation. Soooooooo, I suggest popping all those lovely snacks in a cookie.

QUICK ONE, BUT IT'S TASTY

Blitz the popcorn in a food-processor until roughly ground.

Preheat oven to 180°C/Fan 160°C/Gas 4 and line two baking trays with baking paper.

Cream the butter and both sugars in a large bowl until light and fluffy, add the vanilla and mix again (you can do this in a stand mixer or with a hand-held electric whisk). Add the eggs one at a time, beating after each addition.

Sift the flour, salt and bicarbonate of soda into a separate bowl, then add the flour mixture to the butter and egg mixture. Divide the mixture by three (or by the number of cupboard treats you are using), then add the cupboard treats separately to each portion of dough. Mix well to combine.

"If you fancy a mixture of treats in one cookie, don't worry about dividing up the dough and add all the treats in together instead. This part is up to you, so get creative!"

Using the hinged ice-cream scoop, place portions of the cookie dough on the lined baking trays then gently flatten each scoop. Bake for 12–15 minutes. They should be slightly soft in the middle – you know, the gooey type.

Remove from the oven and leave to firm up on the baking trays for 5 minutes, then place on a wire rack to cool fully.

"It's a bit of a cliché, but for this one get a fat glass of milk and dunk it… you will be in heaven."

Cakes, Bakes, Biscuits

Cinnamon Roll-Ups

neutral oil, for greasing
1 large egg, beaten

Dough
110ml whole milk
100g unsalted butter
1 tsp fine sea salt
250g strong white bread flour
250g plain flour, plus
　　extra for dusting
4 tbsp golden caster sugar
10g fast-action dried yeast
1 tsp ground cinnamon
1 tsp ground cardamom
2 large eggs, beaten
90g tinned pumpkin purée

Filling
75g unsalted butter, softened,
　　plus extra for greasing
150g soft dark brown sugar
¼ tsp freshly grated nutmeg
1 tbsp ground cinnamon
½ tsp ground cloves
100g pecans, roughly chopped

Glaze
165ml Supermalt
250g icing sugar
60ml whole milk
60ml double cream
½ tsp vanilla extract
　　or vanilla bean paste

Who doesn't love a good cinnamon bun. You can't go wrong with slightly enriched dough spread with a cinnamon-spiced butter.

DOUGH I

Warm the milk, butter and salt in a small saucepan over a low heat, stirring constantly, until the butter has melted. Remove from the heat and allow to cool until lukewarm.

Combine the flours, sugar, yeast and spices in a large bowl (a stand mixer bowl, if you have one). Make a well in the mixture, then add the eggs and pour the pumpkin purée into the centre. Pour the lukewarm milk mixture into the bowl, then knead using the stand mixer fitted with the dough hook attachment for 8 minutes. Alternatively, stir everything until it comes together, then knead on a lightly oiled surface until the dough becomes less sticky and elastic.

Shape the dough into a ball and put it into a lightly oiled bowl. Cover with a clean tea towel or some oiled clingfilm and leave to prove at room temperature for 1½–2 hours until the dough has doubled in size.

FILLING × GLAZE

To make the filling, mix the butter and sugar in a bowl with the nutmeg, half of the ground cinnamon and all the ground cloves until it forms a smooth paste. Set aside, with the remaining cinnamon in a separate small bowl.

For the glaze, pour the malted drink into a saucepan and simmer over a medium heat for about 20 minutes until it has reduced to 50ml.

DOUGH II

Lightly grease the muffin tray. Once the dough has risen, flip it out onto a lightly floured surface and roll it out to make a 35 x 25cm rectangle. Spread the spiced sweet butter evenly over the dough with a palette knife or table knife. Finish it off with an even sprinkling of the remaining cinnamon and the chopped pecans.

turn over

Cakes, Bakes, Biscuits

199

With the longest edge closest to you, roll the dough up into a cylinder. Cut into 12 even slices. Place each cinnamon roll in a greased muffin tray hole, cut side down. Place the tray in a large plastic bag, close it loosely and leave to prove at room temperature for a further 50 minutes, or until well risen.

Preheat oven to 200°C/Fan 180°C/Gas 6.

Brush the tops of the buns with beaten egg and bake for 15–20 minutes, or until they are dark golden brown. Remove from the oven, place the tray on a wire rack and allow to cool slightly. Combine all the ingredients for the glaze in a large bowl, including the reduced malted drink, and whisk until slightly thick.

FINISH
Slather each bun generously with the glaze and allow it to set.

"Nah, just eat it."

Cola Bowling Éclairs

Cola Syrup
1 litre cola
1½ tbsp liquid glucose

Choux
100g salted butter
250ml water
200g plain flour
4 or 5 large eggs

Filling
400g mascarpone
4 tbsp icing sugar
2 tsp vanilla extract
    or vanilla bean paste
¼ tsp ground cinnamon
¼ tsp ground nutmeg
¼ tsp ground cloves
1 tsp fine sea salt
6 tbsp cola syrup (see above)
500ml double cream
100g cherry conserve
50g popping candy

Glaze
600g icing sugar
2 tbsp liquid glucose
130ml water
bright red food-colouring gel

Embarrassing story alert! I went to a bowling alley with my brother and sister a couple of years ago. It was one of those days where I was determined to bag a strike. I remember it like it was yesterday: I took a sip of my cola before picking up one of the lightest bowling balls. I was 100 per cent focused. I took a couple of paces back, then ran up to the famous line you can't pass. Did I make it to that line though? Nope. Because I slipped and ripped my trousers. Had to wrap my jacket around me like a massive nappy until I got home. And through all of that, the taste of cola was lingering. Ever since I first tried a coke float, I've wanted to transfer the idea into a bake. I really enjoyed playing with traditional flavour and texture combinations in this recipe. And, dare I say, cherry cola could be tastier than the original? Behold the Cola Éclair.

Preheat oven to 230°C/Fan 210°C/Gas 8 and line a large baking sheet with a silicone mat or baking paper.

OOOO, THAT TASTES LIKE COLA
First, make the cola syrup. Pour the cola into a medium saucepan and place over a medium-high heat. Bring to the boil, then reduce the heat to low, add the liquid glucose and simmer gently for 30 minutes, until the syrup becomes thick and glossy (you need 6 tablespoons for the éclairs). Remove from the heat and leave to cool to room temperature.

CHOUX TIME
While the cola syrup reduces, make the choux. Put the butter in a large saucepan with the water and place over a medium-low heat. Heat until the butter has completely melted and the mixture starts to boil.

As soon as the mixture begins to boil, tip in the flour and reduce the heat. Using a wooden spoon, beat the mixture until it comes away from the sides of the pan and forms a ball. Keep the pan on the heat until the pastry is dry enough to form an even but thin film on the bottom of the pan.

Remove the pan from the heat and transfer the dough to a stand mixer fitted with the beater attachment. Beat on a low speed until most of the steam has evaporated, then one at a time, add the first 4 eggs, beating well after each addition, until the mixture is very smooth and forms a gentle "V" shape when lifted. If necessary, beat the fifth egg in a bowl and add it, little by little, until you reach the right consistency – you may not need it all.

turn over

PIPE THOSE PINS

Transfer the choux mixture to the large piping bag fitted with the nozzle. Pipe 14 bowling-pin-shaped lengths of choux on the lined baking sheet – each one should be 15cm long. Use a wet finger to dab any little points of pastry and smooth out the buns.

Reduce the oven temperature to 170°C/Fan 150°C/Gas 3. Place the buns in the oven and sprinkle them with a few drops of water, then close the oven door and bake for 20 minutes. After 20 minutes, open the oven door to let out the steam, then close it again straight away and bake the buns for a further 10–15 minutes, until they are light golden brown.

Remove the baking sheet from the oven and turn off the heat, then place the buns on a wire rack until they are cool enough to handle. Split each bun in half fully then place the halves back on the tray and into the cooling oven with the door closed. Leave to dry out for another 10–15 minutes while you make the filling and glaze.

COLA FILLING

Beat the mascarpone in a large bowl until smooth, then add the icing sugar, vanilla, spices, salt and the cooled cola syrup, and mix to combine.

In another bowl, whip the cream until it forms soft peaks, then fold it into the mascarpone mixture and spoon the filling into one of the disposable piping bags. Set aside.

COLA CAN GLAZE

To make the glaze, tip the icing sugar and glucose into a medium saucepan with the water and place over a low heat. Stir until the mixture reaches 32–33°C on the sugar thermometer, then pour two-thirds of the mixture into a heatproof large, shallow bowl, and the remaining third into another heatproof bowl. Colour the larger portion of icing red with the food-colouring gel and leave the smaller white.

ASSEMBLE

Remove the buns from the oven. Dip the top half of each one into the red icing, setting each aside on a wire rack as you dip the next.

Fill the remaining piping bag with a small amount of cherry conserve, snip a 1cm hole in the tip and pipe the conserve into the bottom half of each bun. Snip 1cm off the end of the mascarpone filling piping bag and pipe 5 or 6 small dollops on top of the conserve. Sprinkle with popping candy.

Put the rest of the pale icing in a piping bag with a tiny snipped hole and pipe 2 thin horizontal lines of white icing across the thin part of the pins and the numbers from 1–10 underneath.

"You gotta work quickly so that the white lines don't become too thick and heavy."

Place the decorated lids on the filled bottom halves of the éclairs, and you're ready to serve.

Doughnut Dynamite!

Dynamite Dough
500g strong white bread flour,
    plus extra for dusting
2 tbsp activated charcoal
50g caster sugar
10g fine sea salt
10g fresh yeast
75ml lukewarm water
75ml whole milk
4 large eggs
1 tbsp vanilla extract
    or vanilla bean paste
125g unsalted butter, softened

Ammunition Fillin'
3 Pink Lady apples
juice of ½ lemon
1 tsp ground cinnamon
6 plums, halved and stoned
100g fresh blackberries
100ml brandy
juice of 1 pink grapefruit
1 pared strip of grapefruit zest
40g soft light brown sugar
knob of unsalted butter
½ tbsp cornflour

Dynamite Powder
300g caster sugar
2 tbsp activated charcoal
30g popping candy

To Fry × Finish
sunflower oil, for deep-frying
20 mini sparklers

It's Bonfire Night, baby. Whoa, that's come around so fast. So that means fireworks, fried treats and, most importantly, flavour upon flavour. But how can I combine all those three together? DOUGHNUT DYNAMITE. Charcoal doughnuts, the most winter-warming filling you can imagine and a popping-candy sugar coating because… Guy Fawkes, init. The activated charcoal is easy to get hold of – you can purchase it online. Start making the doughnuts the day before you want to serve them.

DAY I

IN D-MINUS DOUGH…

Put all the ingredients for the dough (crumbling in the yeast), apart from the butter, into the bowl of a stand mixer fitted with the beater attachment. Mix the dough on a medium speed for 10 minutes, or until the dough forms a ball and comes away from the sides of the bowl. Turn off the mixer and let the dough rest for 5 minutes.

Start the mixer up again on a medium speed and slowly add the butter to the dough, about 20g at a time.

Once all the butter is incorporated, increase the speed to high for 5–7 minutes, until the dough is glossy and super elastic.

Cover the bowl with clingfilm and leave to prove at room temperature for around 2 hours until it has doubled in size, then knock the dough back. Re-cover with clingfilm and put in the fridge to chill overnight.

DAY II

THE FILLING
Preheat oven to 200°C/Fan 180°C/Gas 6.

Core and peel the apples, cut them into 12 slices each, then toss in a dish with the lemon juice and ground cinnamon.

Place the apples, plums and blackberries in a roasting tin (place the plums cut side up). Mix the brandy and grapefruit juice together then pour it over the fruit. Tuck the strip of zest under the fruit and sprinkle over the sugar. Roast for 20–25 minutes until the fruit has coloured and the juices have started to caramelise.

turn over

Remove from the oven and drain the juice from the cooked fruits through a sieve set over a saucepan. Add that knob of butter and the cornflour to the pan, mix, and cook for 20–25 minutes until reduced and thickened. Pour the thickened juice back over the fruits. Blitz in a food-processor or blender briefly, to make a coarse purée, then set aside until ready to fill.

DYNAMITE POWDER
Combine all the ingredients in a large bowl ready for your fried doughnuts.

SHAPE UP YOUR DOUGH
Once your dough has doubled in size, knock it back again, then on a lightly floured surface, weigh it into 50g portions (you should get 20 portions in total).

"Don't eye-ball it. I would be tempted to make a game out of it: closest one to 50g can chill out and enjoy the doughnuts while the other washes up."

Cut out 20 squares of baking paper slightly bigger than the doughnuts. Put each ball on a piece of baking paper, so it has space to prove and expand.

Lightly sprinkle all the doughnuts with flour, cover them loosely with clingfilm and leave to prove again at room temperature for about 1 hour, or until doubled in size. Check them every now and again, as they will grow on you and you won't even realise.

FRYING
Now it's time for frying. Pour sunflower oil in the deep-fat fryer up to the safety markers and heat to 180°C. Line a tray with kitchen paper.

When the oil has reached the right temperature and your doughnuts have risen, carefully place 2 or 3 doughnuts in your fryer (don't worry about the baking paper, it will float off and you can easily take it out with some metal tongs). Fry for 4 minutes, flipping them with metal tongs or two wooden skewers after 2 minutes so they cook evenly.

Using your tongs, pick out your doughnuts and place them on the paper-lined tray to absorb the excess oil, then toss them in the dynamite powder and pop on a large tray ready to be filled.

Repeat this process until all your doughnuts are fried and coated.

FILL
Poke a decent-sized hole in each doughnut and fill it with the cooked fruits (use a piping bag if you have one).

Okay, this is where you can make a scene. Pop a sparkler in each... 5... 4... 3... 2... 1... DOUGHNUT DYNAMITE!

Shellin' Spread Cannolis

Shells
600g plain flour, plus
    extra for dusting
½ tsp bicarbonate of soda
½ tsp ground cinnamon
½ tsp fine sea salt
100g caster sugar
120ml marsala
2 large egg yolks, plus
    1 egg white
120ml unsalted butter,
    melted and cooled
sunflower oil, for deep-frying

Filling
400g blanched hazelnuts
100g icing sugar, plus
    extra for dusting
400g ricotta
100g mascarpone
100g Biscoff spread
3 tbsp hazelnut spread
½ tsp ground cinnamon
1 tsp vanilla extract
    or vanilla bean paste
100g dark chocolate,
    broken into pieces

Between you and me, this was the last recipe I wrote for the book. So, I thought to myself, why don't I use flavours that I genuinely love – Biscoff spread and hazelnut spread – and place them in a small shell of light crispiness. WOOP!

SHELLS
Sift your flour, bicarbonate of soda, cinnamon and salt into a large bowl, add the caster sugar, and mix well.

Pour the marsala into a smaller bowl, then add the egg yolks followed by the melted butter.

Make a well in the middle of your bowl of dry ingredients and pour in the marsala mixture. Mix with a wooden spoon until well combined.

Turn your mixture onto a lightly floured surface and knead until it forms a smooth and pliable dough, then wrap it in clingfilm and leave it on your work surface to rest for 30 minutes.

Preheat oven to 200°C/Fan 180°C/Gas 6.

FILLING
Place your hazelnuts on a baking tray and roast for 10 minutes.

While the nuts are roasting, sift the icing sugar into a bowl, then beat in the ricotta, mascarpone, Biscoff spread, hazelnut spread, ground cinnamon and vanilla. Cover the bowl of filling with clingfilm and place in the fridge.

Remove the nuts from the oven and leave them on the tray on a wire rack to cool.

ROLL
Clear your work surface then set up your pasta rolling machine at one end. Lightly dust the other end of your working surface with flour.

You also want to set up your deep-fat fryer. Pour sunflower oil in the deep-fat fryer up to the safety markers and heat to 180°C. Line a tray with kitchen paper.

Beat the egg white in a bowl.

turn over

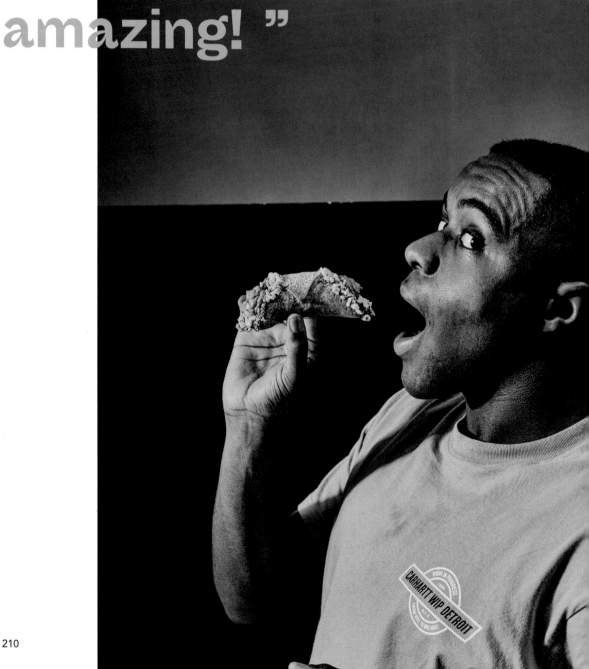

"When something is shellin', it means it's absolutely amazing!"

While the oil is heating up, divide the dough into quarters, re-wrapping 3 of the quarter pieces in clingfilm. Using a rolling pin, roll your first dough quarter to a 5mm-thick rectangle.

Pass the rectangle of dough through the pasta machine on the widest setting, then fold the dough in half and roll it through again. Reduce the thickness-setting on the machine by one and pass it through again. Continue to do this until the dough reaches a thickness of 3mm. Keep your work surface lightly dusted with flour throughout.

Lay the rolled dough on the work surface. Repeat with the remaining quarter pieces of dough, placing each strip of rolled-out dough under a tea towel to prevent it from drying out. Using a 10cm square cutter, chomp out 15–20 squares. Wrap each dough square around a cannoli tube and brush the join with a little egg white at the seam, where they slightly overlap.

FRY
Once the oil has reached 180°C, carefully lower your cannoli tubes into the oil and fry them in batches for 1 minute, or until golden brown and crisp. Remove your cannoli tubes using tongs, ensuring you drain the excess oil back into the fryer.

Gently place the cannolis on the paper-lined tray to absorb more oil, leave them to cool slightly and, once they are cool enough to touch, carefully slide them off the tubes. Place them on a baking tray ready to use. This recipe make more cannolis than you need, so that if you break some, you have a few spare. Pick your best shells to fill.

ASSEMBLE
Blitz the roasted nuts in a food-processor until they are roughly crushed, then fold half of them into your filling and place the rest in a separate bowl.

Melt the dark chocolate in a heatproof bowl over a pan of barely simmering water (making sure the bowl doesn't touch the water), or in a microwave in 20-second bursts, stirring occasionally.

Dip both ends of each cannoli shell in the melted chocolate, then dip both ends in the blitzed nuts.

Spoon your filling into the disposable piping bag, snip the corner of the bag and begin to fill the cannolis. Once they are filled, dust a little icing sugar over the top.

Index

Page numbers in italics refer to photographs

Index

219

Metric/Imperial Conversion Chart

All equivalents are rounded, for practical convenience

WEIGHT

25g	1 oz
50g	2 oz
100g	3½ oz
150g	5 oz
200g	7 oz
250g	9 oz
300g	10 oz
400g	14 oz
500g	1 lb 2 oz
1 kg	2¼ lb

VOLUME (liquids)

5ml	1 tsp
15ml	1 tbsp
30ml	1 fl oz ⅛ cup
60ml	2 fl oz ¼ cup
75ml	⅓ cup
120ml	4 fl oz ½ cup
150ml	5 fl oz ⅔ cup
175ml	¾ cup
250ml	8 fl oz 1 cup
1 litre	1 quart 4 cups

VOLUME (dry ingredients — an approximate guide)

Butter

225g	1 cup (2 sticks)

Rolled oats

100g	1 cup

Fine powders (e.g. flour)

125g	1 cup

Breadcrumbs (fresh)

50g	1 cup

Fine breadcrumbs (dried)

125g	1 cup

Nuts (e.g. almonds)

125g	1 cup

Seeds (e.g. chia)

160g	1 cup

Dried fruit (e.g. raisins)

150g	1 cup

Dried legumes (large, e.g. chickpeas)

170g	1 cup

Grains, granular goods and small dried legumes (e.g. rice, quinoa, sugar, lentils)

200g	1 cup

Grated cheese

100g	1 cup

LENGTH

1cm	½ inch
2.5cm	1 inch
20cm	8 inches
25cm	10 inches
30cm	12 inches

OVEN TEMPERATURES

Celsius	Fahrenheit
140	275
150	300
160	325
180	350
190	375
200	400
220	425
230	450

Thanks

Bloody caramel! Well, there we have it. The second book... in just two years... I can't believe it!

The first one was hard to live up to. But thanks to my family, friends and all the people who continue to inspire me, we made it happen.

More than anything, I want to say thank you to you guys for taking the time to join me on my second cookbook journey. I really hope you use this book as a base for ideas, but then just run with it. EXPRESS YOURSELF.

As always, if you need any help with the recipes, just contact me on my socials: @LiamcBakes on Twitter and Instagram.

Third book, you say? Shh, it's loading :-p Until then, get baking x cooking, and don't forget to show me your creations!

Big love

Liam xx

There's a picture in my first book, *Cheeky Treats*, that lines up with a picture in this book. Have you found it yet?

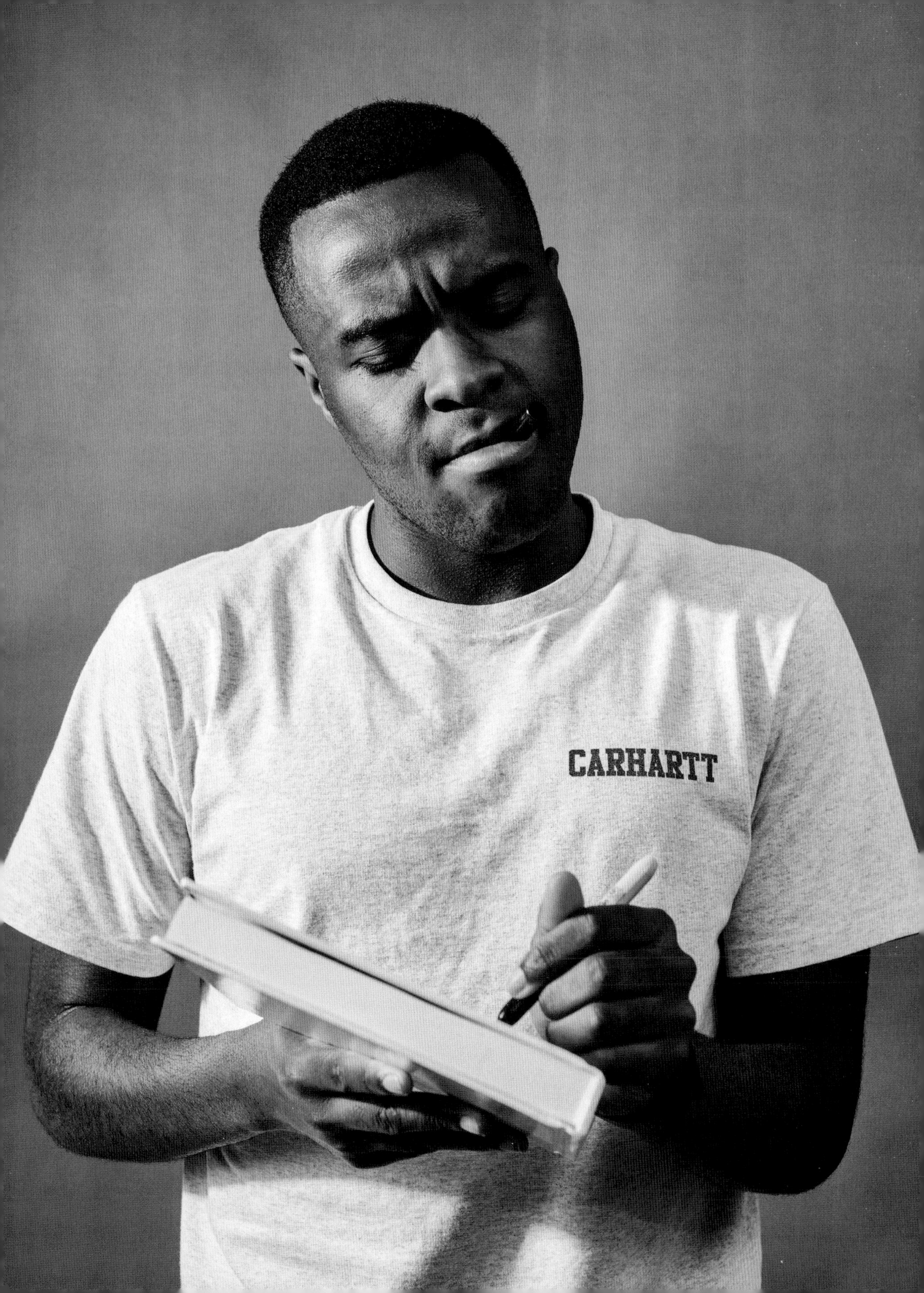
CARHARTT

First published in Great Britain in 2019
by Hodder & Stoughton
An Hachette UK company

1

Copyright © Liam Charles 2019
Photography by Haarala Hamilton © Hodder & Stoughton
2019

A CIP catalogue record for this title is available
from the British Library.

Hardback ISBN 978 1 529 30363 6
eBook ISBN 978 1 529 30362 9

Editorial Director: Nicky Ross
Project Editor: Natalie Bradley
Copy-editor: Laura Nickoll
Design: Studio Polka
Photographers: Liz and Max Haarala Hamilton
Food Stylists: Sam Dixon and Katy Ross
Art Director and Prop Stylist: Anna Wilkins
Production Manager: Claudette Morris

Colour origination by Born Group
Printed and bound in Germany by Mohn Media GmbH

Hodder & Stoughton policy is to use papers that are natural,
renewable and recyclable products and made from wood
grown in sustainable forests. The logging and manufacturing
processes are expected to conform to the environmental
regulations of the country of origin.

The publisher would like to thank iyouall (www.iyouall.com)
and Bert & May (www.bertandmay.com) for supplying the
props detailed below.
iyouall: gold spoons (page 66); green board (page 68);
round board (page 90); glass (centre, page 94); enamel
mugs (page 117); champagne saucers (page 160).
Bert & May: Santona & Luna Dusk tiles (page 169).

Hodder & Stoughton Ltd
Carmelite House
50 Victoria Embankment
London EC4Y 0DZ
www.hodder.co.uk